I0510397

Forex Trading for Beginners

The Ultimate Guide to Learn How to Trade Forex like a PRO

How to Analyze Charts with Technical and Fundamental Analysis, Strategies with Risk Management & Psychology

Andrew Stock

Table of Contents

Chapter 1: The Overview of Forex Trading and Its History

FOREX is a short form of Foreign Exchange, and therefore FOREX trading is the exchange of currencies around the world. It is a trade that is referred to as Over the Counter Trade (OTC) because it takes place without a physical place to meet. The buyer and the seller are only connected through telephone, telex, and a communication system. However, there few centers where the trade takes place in fixed places, an example is in Paris and Brussels, where bank representatives meet to bargain and fix rates of popular currencies. In FOREX trade, the major currencies include the US Dollar, the Japanese Yen, and the Euro. The participants in the trade include the central banks, exchange brokers, commercial banks, and corporates. The individual traders are involved in the trade through the exchange brokers.

The history of FOREX trading dates back to the time when World War II ended. After the war, the world started to experience instability in the economy, and most western governments needed to curb the situation. The government, therefore, agreed to have a Bretton Woods System, which was to exchange gold with other currencies. All the currencies were then traded against the US dollar that was set using the value of gold at the time. The situation stabilized for some time, but when the economies started growing at different, the system became limiting for major economies such as the US. The fluctuation rate was limited to a maximum or minimum of 1% compared to the dollar, and any nation that violated this had to control the imbalance through its central bank. The US felt that stopped its transaction using the Bretton Woods System, which brought a crisis that led to the abolishment of the system in 1971. The Bretton Woods System was replaced by another currency valuation system. The new system was different such that unlike the Bretton System, which had fixed rates, it had free-floating rates that were determined by the forces in the market. Individual currencies varied in value, thus increasing the need for exchange and trading. This system is what is still in use for FOREX exchange today. The new system had a problem of determining fair rates of exchange, but they were alleviated later, as the improvement in communication technology made it easier.

Earlier, the FOREX market was operated exclusively by central banks between governments and commercial banks. In the 1980s and 1990s, it was expanded to commodity trading advisors (CTAs), funds, big investors and large corporations. This is because this group of investors was able to adhere to the strict guidelines established for credit by the big banks; smaller investors could not meet the guidelines. In the 2000s, the market grew and gained much recognition by more individuals around the world. The computer technology also grew rapidly during this period, leading to the emergence of online FOREX trading, which is done through brokers.

The online FOREX brokers create a credit line with a bank that is involved in the trade to enable access to currencies for trade. The trade now involves small volumes of currencies, contrary to the earlier trading system that required individuals to have large sums of money to trade in large volumes. Today, investors are more rigorous and seek to diversify their trading portfolios to draw more returns.

The FOREX trade is in the financial market together with stock trading and others. However, it is different from the other trades in the financial market, such that you do not need to use a centralized exchange that has only one price for a particular currency, at a given time. It is made up of different dealers that have different rates, making the market overwhelming, but amazing because it has so many choices. Competition between the many dealers is fierce, and getting the best deal is something that happens all the time. Another good thing about FOREX is that you can trade anywhere; you are not restricted to certain markets like in the case of stock trading.

The market has many dealers, as mentioned earlier, but they are organized on a ladder. At the top of the market, the ladder is interbank, which is composed of the world largest banks and some of the smaller banks. Traders at this level trade with each other directly through Reuters Dealing or the Electronic Brokerage Services (EBS). From the interbank going down the ladder, next is the hedge funds, retail market makers, and corporations; this group does its transactions through commercial banks. Therefore their rates are higher than those of interbank. At the lower part of the ladder are the retail traders, who include individuals who are small scale traders.

FOREX trading is one of the trades that bring earning to a country; the more the responsible traders a country has, the more it earns from the exchange. Entry in this form of trade is always a good choice of investment, as there are no commissions of trading like the other forms of trade. There are no government fees, exchange or clearing fees. There are also no brokerage fees as most brokers are compensated through the "spread." The only cost incurred is the transaction fee, which is low; it ranges from 0.07% to 0.1 where the lowest is for larger transactions. The FOREX trade also has no limit like in the case of stock and features, your size of the trade is determined by the amount of money you have for investment in the trade. The FOREX is a 24-hour market; it does not wait for opening time or bell and does not depend on the day of the week or month. Which makes it suitable for all people, including part-time traders? The market also attracts everyone because of its easy entry; when compared to other financial market trades, FOREX requires a minimum of $25 and allows individuals to have mini and micro-accounts for trading. The market welcomes all people, but no individual, institution, or company can control the market price, because it is so huge. This form of trade has high liquidity because the market is so huge and accessible that anytime you want to buy or sell; there is always someone willing to exchange.

When trading, one currency is exchanged with another, for instance, when you exchange the Dollars with the Euros, you say you are trading Dollars for Euros. The earning comes in when the money you traded with fluctuates in value over time. The rule is always, buy when it is low, and sell when it is high. However, it is not easy to determine how low is low and how high is high; to determine the low and high therefore one needs know the factors influencing the rate of the currency in order to predict the rate of the currency in the future. The difference between the rate of selling and that of buying a currency is known as the "spread" and it is expressed in "pips." A Pip is the smallest unit of any currency.

It is not easy to predict a market trend, and therefore are methods used to guide the prediction. These methods are the technical analysis and fundamental analysis. The fundamental analysis consists of policies put forth by a country that affects the currency. The central bank of each nation has a responsibility for the well-being of a nation, and therefore, it analyses the factors that affect the economy and make policies that improve the status of the economy. It is therefore important to look at the adjustment in the policy of the country of the currency you want to trade with and regular announcement because they are the economic indicators that bring about changes in the FOREX market. The indicators include interest rates, the GDP, consumer price index, and industrial production, among others

The technical analysis concentrates on market trends, trying to see if the current trend of the currency can reverse, and if it does, how the market will respond to the changes in the future. It looks at the history of the price of currencies and volumes traded, through reading and interpreting graphs. Mathematical tools used in making technical analysis include gaps and trends, waves, and number theory. The technical analysis uses three basic assumptions: history repeats itself, prices move in trends and market discounts everything.

For one to have a reasonable profit from the FOREX trading it is good to have a good risk management plan. However, the management should be based on capital preservation; remember that you cannot trade without funds in your account. Making big profits is not bad, but it is good to have a calculated risk. It is better to have a little success rate than to risk much and lose it all.

An investor should also have a trading plan to make sure that he or she achieves the set goals. The plan should not just be written down, it should be followed just the way you plan to buy household items; always buy when the prices are low and when your prediction about the rising of prices has a higher chance of being true. And sell when your prediction that the price might fall as a high probability that it will happen. There is no proper action to FOREX trading; it is having a good plan that is based on good analysis.

Chapter 2: Advantages of Forex Trading Flexible

There is high flexibility for the persons involved in the trade when it comes to trading goods as well as services. You are not restricted or limited to the amount of money to use while trading. There are no excess rules as well as regulations that have been put in place to be followed by the ones involved in trading. It is as well a market that operates for twenty-four hours and throughout the week. Hence, it is wise considering as a part-time engagement by anyone who does a regular job since it has no time restriction. You don't have to wait for the market to open, and as well the market doesn't sleep. You have the freedom to choose when and at what time you want to get into trading. You are no restrictions for you to waiting for a specific session to trade as it is the case with trading stock. You get into the trade when you have the time to do that. It is always in operation since it is not affected by any situation. You can get updates anytime you need and as well get to view the trend when you have time to see. The different trading styles will enable you to trade at your convenience. If you intend to take the position for a short duration, Forex trading is an excellent opportunity for you. It is the easily accessible market to any trader.

There is high liquidity

There are high numbers of the people involved in the foreign exchange market compared to any financial market. Despite its significant size, it is as well extremely liquid. Because of the high liquidity, big players get attracted to Forex trading. It, in turn, leads to filling the gap of the big orders of money trade with either small or no price deviation. Efficient pricing is promoted since there is no price manipulation, as well as no deviation, is experienced, from the actual price. Under the apparent market conditions, you can buy as well as sell any time since there are always people who are ready to trade. There are constant price patterns throughout the trade despite the level of volatility. The high liquidity makes the Forex market efficient, and the heat of competition not felt. It is so despite the high number of traders involved on either side. The significant number of persons engaged in the trade ensures there are always transactions going on in the market. You will be lucky to get an opportunity because the prices do not shift dramatically. Transactions are completed quickly as well as efficiently, and hence the spread, as well as the transaction costs accrued, are relatively low. You can make suppositions of the price movement in the market.

Central Exchange is not involved

The central exchange interferes with the market in rare cases or either in extreme conditions. It is a guarantee that there will be no cases of prices dropping or either price manipulation. That serves as an advantage to anyone who wants or has invested in Forex trading. The market does not experience changes as it is the case into the markets that trade in equity shares and many others. There are no regulators since trade is conducted over-the-counter in the entire globe. The central banks interfere in exceptional cases, and this rarely happens. Localizing, as well as deregulating the market aids in avoiding those interferences.

Volatility

You can easily change to a different currency if there are higher profits or either good investment associated with it. There are higher risks associated with investing in the money-driven market. But volatility provides significant benefits by changing from one currency to another, which yields a good return. It makes it an advantage to lower the risk factors involved as well as increase the profit. You can get some benefit once you speculate on the price changes, either rising or falling. The Forex trading gives maximum grasp compared to any other financial investing trade out there. It serves as an added advantage to level your investment. The exchange rates are very lively, and profit can be gained anytime when the prices shift anytime you are willing. You require a short duration for you to open as well as closed positions. High volatility attracts opportunities to make huge profits.

Low barriers in case you want to enter the market

To invest in being a currency trader, you are not required to have a vast amount of money. You can quickly get into Forex trading even with little initial capital. To have a trading account, you are required to have a deposit of $25 as a minimum. Compared to future, options as well as trading stock, which requires you to have the right amount of money. It is relatively cheap since a large amount of capital associated with opening an account does not apply in this case. Hence, it is more accessible to an average person who is interested and does not have much money for a start. The trading to attracts traders with different experience levels, and hence, experience does not serve as a barrier to enter into currency trading. For a person entering the market for the first time, there are no many risks involved. They can test, improve as well as organize their new skills, which later turns to be a future benefit.

Different methods can be used to trade

The trading method that you will prefer, you will be provided with an opportunity by the Forex market. The advantage associated is you can buy as well as sell currencies according to specific responses. The world events taking place within a particular location or either change in the economy can be a determinant. You can as well base on the history of price patterns, and hence, you can identify the trends. Currency linked to an economy known to sustain it. You can as well put several views together to come up with a trade-picking approach that is unique. Forex trading is put to use in several trading plan categories. Whether you have a short-term or a long-term goal, Forex trading will not disappoint you in any way. They have a lot to offer to you as a small beginner.

Leverage will make your finances go further

A contract for differences subjected under a force will make your money go for a long duration. You are then in a position to pay a small portion of the entire value. Profits, as well as losses, made the aggregate value on the time of closure. Doing trade on the margin will give you an opportunity to reaping a good profit even from your small investment. You will are equipped with tools to manage risks, including price alerts, as well as running balances. You are allowed to several strategic positions as a way to curb unwanted risks. Hedging serves as a right approach of mitigating as well as limiting losses to a considerable and known amount. You can choose Forex pairs, and when failures occur on one pair, the other set in a different position can mitigate. Making a small deposit will help you control an immense contract value. You will reap enticing profits as well as minimize risking capital. You can trade with substantial cash flow compared to your deposit. Choose a reasonable leverage size which will translate to getting a potential profit as well as reducing the losses that you may incur.

You can access tools to aid you in trading

There are numerous trading platforms on tablets, mobile, web, and many more. You can also access a specialist platform in case you want to take your trading on a higher level. There are a lot of trademarks designed to assist you in upgrading your trading and interactive charts as well as consolidated news feeds. Some of the features include stops as well as limits that are vital in managing risks. You will too access products that are designed to assist you in growing the Forex trading. You will be offered to help you practice trading as well as improve your skills. The demo accounts serve as a variable resource in case you are financially down, and you need to sharpen your trading techniques. You will establish whether it is safe for you to open a live marketing account.

Wide range of options

When you buy one currency, you are likely to sell the other meaning that the transactions should be in pairs. There are numerous options you can put into consideration in Forex trading. You can trade in multiple pairs by choosing the set based on specific criteria. You can either decide to base on volatility patterns as well as the level of economic development. It is as well advisable to time when it is convenient. Embrace volatility, and this will help you to shift from on to another currency pair. When you speculate that the value of a particular currency will decline, you have to sell that and then buy one which to pair with it. Forex trading provides a wide range of opportunities to trade and not forgetting the budget as well as the risk factor. You sell one currency and buy the other. A Forex pair cost is similar to a unit of the money purchased and worth in the selling currency. You will make a profit or loss depending on the accuracy of the prediction you have made. In either case, you are subject to make a profit regardless of the deviation of the market.

The is no fixed amount for you to operate with

In many markets, the contract, as well as lot sizes, are regulated and supposed to be a certain amount. There are no such restrictions in the currency market, and you have the freedom to operate with the amount you are willing to. A reasonable cost is involved in providing you with a great option. It is pretty consistent when it comes to trading as well as investing. It is so because both the buyer and the seller are directly involved in eliminating any broker that can be required.

The cost is low

There are typically considerate transaction costs involved under usual market conditions. The Forex trading is associated with a little expense since there are rare cases of brokerage as well as commissions given. It is more reliable compared to any other type of trade where you take into account brokerage fees. The cost you are supposed to pay to the Forex broker is relatively small compared to what is paid to get into trading other securities. There are no clearing as well as government fees that need to be deductions.

Individual control

One of the critical advantages of Forex trading is that any trader has total control in either buying or selling. You are not forced to make a trade that you are not in agreement. You as well have the freedom to make the final decision whether you are willing to get into trading. You will get a chance to access to the extent you are ready to risk for you to earn money.

There is transparency in any information issued

You can easily access information concerning rates as well as the current forecast since it is accessible to all the public. The period that is involved for any information to be distributed makes the trading fairly judged. It happens in such a short time despite the large market size.

Confidence increase

When you get to the jackpot, your confidence will increase. It will automatically create goodwill, and you become active in trading money, which in turn creates traffic.

Do not emotionally invest in the organization you are trading on behalf. It makes it hard for you to do away with the position even in cases where the market does not go to plan. Forex trading is an excellent idea to help you detach from such emotion and as well is essential for making the trading success. There are no emotions associated with any spillage that occurs along the way.

Chapter 3: How to Trade Forex

Trading Forex can be a very interesting hobby for other people in the current world. This form of a thrilling kind of hobby can be a great source of generating revenue. To lighten up peoples light, over five trillion US dollars are traded in a day. To formally understand the trade, the process is divided into three namely learning basics terminologies in Forex, opening of an online Forex brokerage account and starting the trade.

Learning Basic Terminologies in Forex

1. Understanding basic Forex terminology

The first two terminologies an individual is supposed to understand are the base currency and quote currency. During the Forex trade, two currencies are always traded. The currency that is being got rid is referred to as the base currency. The other currency being bought is known as the quote currency. For a person to buy the quote currency, he or she will be guided by the foreign exchange rates. The foreign exchange rates help a person to know how much he or she will have to spend.

There are two positions in the process of trading currencies. A person can choose to take a long term or short term position. A long term position involves a person buying the base currency and in turn selling the quote currency. On the other hand, buying the base currency and selling the base currency is referred to a trader taking a short term position. The trader always has a price which he or she can willingly buy the base currency in exchange to get quote currency. This price is always known as a bid fee.

Bid prices can change during the process of broking currencies. This leads to the rise of an asking price. It is the price an individual is able to sell the base currency in return to gain the quote currency. Bid price mostly is the best price available in the market a person can buy the other currency. The difference between the asked price and the bid price is known as a spread.

2. Reading the Forex quote

There are two numbers an individual will observe in the Forex quote. The numbers present include the bid price and the asking price. The bid price is always situated on the left side while the asking price is always situated on the right side.

3. Descending on what currency a person wants to buy and sell

This process starts with a person predicting an economy. An individual can take a common economy like the United States of America economy. An individual can believe of the US economy declining. This situation is bad for the American dollar since it will depreciate in terms of value. Therefore, the situation will lead to a person offloading the dollar in exchange for the other forms of currency which strong economies.

The individual can look at a country trading position to know which currency to buy and sell. The better country to look at is that with a high amount of goods that are inconsistent demand. There are high possibilities for such a country to have high numbers of exports and thus make more money from international and local trade. The phenomenon will be a strong boost to a country and in turn, boosting the currency. The information favoring such a country gives a trader the best currency to invest in.

The decision over which currency to buy and sell can be determined by the political temperatures of a country. The most crucial times are during the elections in a country. The currency is approximated to rise if a person winning the election has an agenda aligning to favorable fiscal policies. The currency can be favorable to buy if the regulations on economic growth are loosened. The action likely leads to an increase in the value of a country's currency.

Economic reports of a country can also help a person in making the decision on which currency to buy and sell. An individual can choose to focus on a country's Gross Domestic Income or a country's Per Capita Income. Other information that can be critical includes the employment rate and inflation rate. This critical information will provide a trader with accurate information about the value of the currency to buy and sell.

4. Learning how to calculate profits

The process involves a person's ability to be able to measure the value change in two currencies. Pip measures the difference between the two traded currencies. One pip is usually equated to 0.0001change in value. A good example can be drawn from an exchange of the Euro to the American dollar. If the trade of EUR/USD shifts from 2.646 to 2.647, the value of the currency is said to have increased by ten pips. The next step involves an individual multiply the pips numbers his or her account with the current exchange rates. The value got will help an individual know if he has made a gain or a decrease in his account.

Opening of Online Forex Brokerage Account

1. Researching of different brokerages

There are several factors an individual is supposed to consider while choosing his or her brokerage. These factors to be kept in consideration include:

- Going out for the experience. This should be the main consideration when choosing a brokerage individual or a company. The person or company is decided on is supposed to have a minimum experience of ten years in the market. The experience will be able to help a person to know the company is on track. Experience also indicates the company or an individual is good at taking care of his or her clients.

- One is supposed to ensure that the brokerage is regulated. The regulation of brokerages is mostly done by the chief oversight body. It is very pleasing if a broker chose on has a total submission to the government. The situation gives an individual reassurance on broker transparency and honesty. There are several oversight bodies across the globe and they include;
    a. United Kingdom; Financial Conduct Authority
    b. Switzerland; Swiss Federal Banking Institution.
    c. Australia; Australian Securities and Investment Commission.
- The types of available products by the broker are also another factor for an individual to consider. There are some factors that help an individual to know if the brokerage has a wide business reach and a large client base. One of the determining factors these occurrence is also trading securities and commodities.
- A person interested in the forex market is supposed to be a careful reader of reviews. It is because some dishonest brokers can write reviews that are false to build a good

brand for themselves. These reviews written help an individual to get the flavor of the broker. However, an individual is supposed to take these brokers with a granule of the brackish.

- Visiting the website of a broker is not supposed to be left out. This website is supposed to have a good professional look. The links provided on the website are supposed to be functional also. If there are any doubts on the website, an individual is supposed to steer clear from the broker.

- Checking on the transactional cost of each trade is also advantageous to a person interested to be successful in Forex trade. An individual is supposed to check how much the bank will charge him or her to wire funds into his or her Forex account.

- An individual is supposed to be able to focus on the essentials. These essentials include focusing on good clientele support and transactions that are easy and transparent. An individual is supposed to be attracted to a broker who has a good reputation.

2. Requesting information about opening an account

There are two forms of account an individual can open to be able to trade in the Forex market. An individual chose to open a personal account or he or she can choose to open a managed account. Having a personal account will help an individual to manage his or her account. On the other hand, having a managed account tasks the broker with the ability to execute the trade on behalf of the individual.

3. Filling out the correct paperwork

There are several ways the appropriate paperwork can be filled. An individual can choose to order the paperwork by mail services. The other method will entail downloading the papers from the internet in the form of a PDF file. The next step will involve an individual checking the transaction charges by the bank for transferring funds to an individual's brokerage account. This fee is important because it affects the profit calculation in the Forex trade.

4. Activation of the account

The most common occurrence entails the broker sending the activation link to an individual's email. The link sent always contains guidelines that help an individual to start.

Starting Trading

1. Analysis of the market

Market analysis is always the first step while starting to trade in the Forex market. There are several ways an individual can use to analyze the market. They include:

I.   Technical analysis; technical analysis entails the use of chats or historical data. These forms will help a Forex trader to be able to predict the movement of currency basing his thought on the previous events. These data can be obtained from several sources. The main form sources include from the brokerage or the MetaTrader which is a common platform for those in the Forex trade.

II.   Fundamental analysis; this form of analysis involves taking a keen look at the key areas in a country's economy. The information got from these fundamental areas form a key to a person trading choices.

III.   Sentimental analysis; this form of market analysis is highly subjective. An individual using this form of market analysis will try to get a good analysis of the market mood. This will enable an individual to know if the market is bullish. It is very difficult to put a finger on the sentiment of the market. However, an individual can be able to make very good guesses that influence his or her trade.

2. Determining an individual's margin

This is highly dependable on the broker's strategy in place. An individual can make investments of small amounts of money and still be able to make huge trades in the Forex market. An example can be used of an individual with a desire to trade one hundred units at one percent margin. This will make the broker put one thousand American dollars in an individual's account to act as security. If an individual makes the gains, it will add in his or her account to its value. On the other hand, loses will deduct from the individual's account from its value. Such occurrences have made individuals invest 2% of the funds in a specific pair currency.

3. Placing of an individual order

An individual at this point can place orders of various kinds. These orders include:

- Market order; this order includes an individual using the market order to instruct his or her broker to buy or sell at the present market rates.
- Limit orders; this point entails an individual instructing his or her broker to trade at a precise price. An individual can sell the currency when it lowers to a certain price or he or she can buy when it gains up to a certain price.
- Stop orders; this order involves two of the options. An individual can decide to buy currency above the present value in the market. On the other hand, an individual can choose to sell currency below the present market value.

4. Watching an individual's profit and loss

At this point, an individual is warned from becoming emotional. It is because the market is very volatile in most cases. An individual is predicted to observe lots of ups and downs. Therefore, one is supposed to be firm with his or her strategy in the market. This will enable him to see profits coming overtime if he or she is confident in his or her strategy.

Chapter 4: Platforms for Investing in Forex

In a bid to understand what the various platforms for Forex are, an individual needs to be equipped with the knowledge of what Forex is. Forex from the face value of it is a combination of the words foreign currency exchange. Foreign currency exchange from its terminologies refers to the process of converting from one currency to another usually for purposes of trade. Other purposes may include tourism and even commerce. Forex happens in the market for foreign exchange because this is the place where the value of currencies is determined. In order to acquire an item of your choice, one needs to have currency. Currency is of key importance since this is the only medium of exchange. Take for instance you are a citizen of the United Kingdom and you wish to acquire clothe wear from The United States, you will have to pay for the clothing wear in dollars rather than sterling pounds.

For this to happen, the importer based in the United Kingdom will have to convert an equivalent amount of sterling pounds into US Dollars. This is because the medium of exchange in the US is limited to US Dollars. The transport industry experiences the same. This mostly happens when it comes to air transport. A United States' tourist coming to Africa to witness the famous Wild beast migration cannot pay dollars to see the animals migrate. He or she will have to convert the currency into one that is favorable. The act of converting one currency to another is governed by a rate known as the currency exchange rate.

The exchange for these currencies from one currency to another has no defined place. This means that these exchange can take place anywhere. The exchange is controlled by a computer network thus enabling the exchange to occur in an over-the-counter manner. Thus OTC. The market operates on a 24hr basis and runs till Saturday noon. Here, curorency exchange takes place on a worldwide perspective. This means that the exchange happens across every time zone. For instance, when commerce day ends in Hong Kong, it commences in the US.

In the past before the onset of Bretton Woods institutions, the currency would be left to float freely and the value of a currency would be determined by the desire of those particular people to engage in trade. Most people do not engage in Forex directly but rather indirectly. They leave their banks to engage in such kind of transactions.

There are three internationally accepted means of trading in Forex. These methods are usually employed by individuals, corporations, and institutions. They include:

- The spot market
- Forwards market
- The future market

The spot market refers to a platform where goods are bought and sold for immediate delivery. The spot market often sets the basis upon which the forwards and futures market ensues. With the introduction of the electronic OTC mode of exchange and the onset of various middlemen in this field, the spot market has been in a booming business since people are always buying and traveling to various parts of the world. In a nutshell, the spot market is where the exchange of currencies occur according to the reigning exchange rates. It has been a common behavior of people mistaking the Forex for the spot market.

The prices and exchange rates in the market are often affected by the curves of supply and demand. There are many aspects that lie beneath the curves of demand and supply. These factors are not limited to economic performance, current interest rates, and political stability. Take for instance the scenario of Somalia. A tourist from the US would not be inclined to visit Somalia because of the various reasons associated with political instability. When the conditions at home do not favor trade, then the Forex in that country drops drastically.

The mentality of how a currency will perform in the future is also a key factor that needs to be taken into consideration. A spot deal is the finality of an agreement of performance. Here, an individual ought to deliver a specified amount of currency to counter the other specified amount of currency. This exchange is usually akin to the reigning exchange rates.

The Forwards and futures markets assume a different kind of path. Whereas the spot market is keen to deal with the current actual currencies, the forwards and futures markets focus on contracts. These particular contracts are often to the effect that a claim towards a particular currency is due. The focus is often on the specific type of currencies and the future date for settlement. For instance, when it comes to the forwards market, two parties come together and determine the terms of the agreement in the contract. They then proceed to purchase a contract in the OTC.

The futures market involves an exchange where one can trade on commodities or financial instruments at an explicit price for delivery at an explicit time in the coming days. Here, future contracts availed on the basis of size and the date upon which the amount will be settled. The US has an association that regulates the futures market. This association is known as the National Futures Association. The future contract contains explicit details which cut across all the factors discussed underneath the contract.

The contracts have a binding effect on the parties in that the parties are obliged to perform their duties to the latter. It is important to note that the contracts can be repurchased or resold before the period of expiry is due. The effect of the forwards and futures market is to shield the corporation o individual against risk.

Forex markets act a shield for firms especially those engaging in businesses in foreign countries. The phobia is often directed towards the rising and falling tides of currency values when they trade in goods outside domestic jurisdictions. Forex markets act as a shield to these kinds of firms through having an already set up timeline that governs the whole transaction. For instance, a trader can purchase or dismiss currencies in anticipation. This then creates an exchange rate that is binding to the particular transaction. This type of arrangement is popular in future markets whereby it is governed by a central authority.

However, there are factors that affect the supply and demand curve for currencies. These factors include political instability, economic strength, and tourism. An increase or decrease in currency value will always mean that there is an opportunity to make a profit. Speculating that one currency's value will diminish is like saying that the other currency's value will dominate. This will lead to pairing. For instance, Japan and the US are paired with speculation that the interest rates will fall in the US (YEN/USD). This means that you will require fewer yen to match up the dollar.

Various Platforms for Investing In Forex

An individual, corporation or company who has the desire to invest in Forex may settle on any of the following channels of investment. On the Forex market, the price of the national currency, for instance, is the way the market views the initial position of the economy. With an initial comprehension of what Forex means, an individual is able to understand that most of these transactions occur online. With that in mind, the various platforms for investing in Forex include:

Commercial and prop platforms are the two major types of trading platforms. Commercial platforms are fashioned to meet the expectations of daily traders, retailers, and investors. Their characteristics involve an easy to use a feature that enables ease of use by any individual. They also encompass other features that may be of aid to the trader such as news reports that may improve the investor's knowledge in the market. The investor knowledge is improved by continuous interaction with such feeds.

Prop platforms occur on a larger basis in that they are fashioned to allow a particular mode and requirement of trading to ensue. In order to settle on a proper trading platform, an individual needs to take note of the following factors: the kind of fees and features that are provided should be a driving factor towards settling on a particular trading platform. Traders who engage the Forex on a daily basis are often inclined to be in need of features that may be of aid to them in making decisions. Before making a decision, one needs a complete in-depth on the issue at hand.

Investors require a candid view of the available options and gaps to exploit. The amount of fees payable is also of great importance since traders will always be inclined to be pulled towards the direction of fewer fees. A scenario where trade-offs will occur should be anticipated. This refers to the compromising of quality or quantity in order to increase on another variable. When you pay fewer fees and thus get lessor information, this will, in turn, take a toll on your whole investment. A number of platforms may be tied to explicit middlemen whereas others are only tied to a particular broker. Thus the reputation of middleman is key when contemplating on which investment road to take. There are other trading platforms that have an already formed threshold. If an individual or corporation seeking to invest does not meet the threshold set, then they do not qualify to invest.

There are numerous trading platforms which surpass even numbers.

The most renowned ones include:

Network of middlemen

They are a channel that allows the sharing of numerous amounts of information across the Forex. They act as pointers to where the business is most favorable. Middlemen will always s be favored by the minimum trade barriers.

Trade Station

This is a type of platform that uses automated scripts to perform trading strategies. It is most popular among algorithmic traders

Robinhood

This type of platform operates on a free-commission manner. This is because this type of platforms makes money from various sources. The sources include interest on cash in its savings.

Metatrader

This is the most popular trading platform. Its key features are that it combines many platforms of middlemen and has a scripting language that is handy when automating Forex.

Interactive Brokers

Interacrive Brokers LLC (IB) is a U.S.-based brokerage firm. It operates the largest electronic trading platform in the U.S by number of daily avarage revenue trades. The company brokers stocks, options, futures, EFPs, futures options, forex, bonds, and funds.

A party trading in Forex will face a lot of challenges. Among these challenges, there will be a bag of goodies. For instance, the Forex markets amerce up to 5 trillion a day. This is a direct fact that they are the giants in terms of volumes of trade daily.

The conversion of one currency to another and the entry and exit from the Forex markets becomes less subtle because all these happen in a fraction of a second. Besides that, a trader needs to understand the importance of leverage. When a bank or a financial lending institution lends trader money, it allows him or her to control a large position when the reality is that there is very little to it that they actually own.

The Forex market operates on a 24-hour basis. This means that you can conduct your business at any time of the day having no setback. In order to trade soundly, a trader needs in-depth on the various factors that affect various shifts. He or she should visualize every key aspect before trading. There are various factors that are inherent in a particular currency and these are usually the factors that control the currency values.

Traders with relatively fewer funds or those trading in fewer amounts of capital have a chance of venturing in the Forex market and becoming successful rather than in other markets. These type of traders should focus on understanding the trends in the Forex market since they engage in exchange daily. Traders with larger funds, such as long-term investors should focus on the tides of the Forex market. An inner comprehension of the requisites of the macroeconomic environment and the factors behind the shift in the currency values will be of great aid to traders seeking to assume Forex trading.

Chapter 5: Pips and what you need to know about them

What Is A Pip?

When you get into the foreign exchange circle, chances are you will encounter the word pip countless times as you begin your journey through the currency trading market. So, what is a pip, and why is it so important in this trade?

In foreign exchange (Forex), pip is the 'point in percentage'. When a currency pair is traded, the pip is what is used to detect losses and gains.

A pip is seen as the basic unit in the Forex market and therefore, for you to be successful in this trade, you will need to understand it. In most currencies, it is represented by the last figure in four decimal places. 0.0003. the three here then is the pip. Therefore, if an exchange rate of the USD to say KSHS is 1 USD = 102.1675, the 5 at the end is the pip.

For example, the US Dollar, probably them the most stable currency in the world and therefore, the currency onto which others are held up against, is often measured on a pip of 0.0001.

There are notable exceptions though, with the Japanese Yen being the most common. The USD pip point against the JPY is often to three decimal places; therefore, the pip is 0.001.

What is The Function of the Pip?

Now, we have stated above that the pip is a basic unit of foreign exchange and therefore, is one of the things you will need to be aware of as you enter the currency trading market. But right now, the question you ask 'Why is the pip and understanding it important?'

Due to fluctuations in the Forex market, the pip was developed to be able to handle the shifts in the exchange rates. Had it been a larger figure, say well into the ones and tens units of measurement, it would greatly affect not just prices in the Forex market, but it would have the potential to cause far-reaching effects, like changes in prices in commodities in the consumer market. if the pip was said, 1, an increase of two would be a huge shift, with the potential to shift economies.

Therefore, by having the pip value low in the decimal figure, they were able to develop a mechanism that would ensure more stability during fluctuations,even though, as we will discover further down the article, it still is a figure that can quickly grow into huge amounts. So, let's look at some of the terms we could encounter in this field.

Ask Price, Bid Price, and Spread: Term You Should Be Familiar With

Once you set foot in the Forex trading world, you will come across several terminologies, and today, right here, we look at some of the most important ones used.

Let's say you want to sell a currency pair. The price you put forth is what we will define as the 'ask' price as the price. The asking price is, then, the price that you would give when buying a currency pair. It is slightly higher than the market price.

The price that you can sell a currency pair is called the bid price. It is often the price put on display in banks and Forex halls. You will find that this bid price is lower than the market price, which will ensure that whoever buys from you sells it at the market price so as to get a profit.

Then, we have spread. If, say, the bid price is 1.9786 and the asking price is 1.9792, the difference of 6 pips (1.9792 - 1.9786) is the spread. So, we can look at spread as the pip difference between a bid and ask price.

In foreign exchange, it is important to note that Forex happens with two pairs of currencies, where one sells one to buy another. they are called currency pairs

For example, if you have the GBP (Great Britain Pound) and wants to change it with the USD, this will be called trading the USD/GBP pair. Therefore, when you give your GBP to get the USD, you will be selling the GBP and buying the USD.

Popular Currency Pairs in Trading

So, now you think, in order to make the right risks, what popular currency pairs do I need to be aware of?

Popular currency pairs will often be from more developed countries. This is because, since they have more stable economies, their currencies are subjected to less volatility and manipulation due to very small pip values between their exchange rates. They tend to also have more political stability, thus making their markets more certain, and thus, trading in their currencies less risky than others. You will then find that these currencies become the most traded and often, the pairing of one stable currency to another becomes more popular and less risky. But, as it is said, in the Forex business, the risk is the name of the game.

Examples of some of the most popular currency pairs are GBP/USD (British Pound and the US Dollar, USD/JPY (The US Dollar and the Japanese Yen), EUR/USD

As seen from above, the US Dollar is seen to be the most stable, occurring in most of the common currency pair. It is the most stable currency in the world, which is why you can conduct business using US Dollars in pretty much any country in the world. It often has a low spread when traded with others hence its popularity. However, other common pairs could include GBP/JPY, EUR/GBP. These are referred to as Cross currencies, so defined because they do not feature the USD.

Then, there are the so-called exotic pairs. This is the currency pairs between the developing world, as they are colloquially known. Because of their instability, they are more volatile and therefore, are often considered riskier to trade. This is also influenced by the political temperatures, which often has wide implications in the market certainty/uncertainty. An example of this pair could be the USD/KSHS

How Do I Calculate Pips?

Now to the math.

To get the value of the pip, you will need to divide 1/10,000 or 0.0001 (the pip is calculated to the fourth decimal) by the exchange rate. As noted earlier, this is an exception when you are trading the USD, or the EUR with the Japanese Yen, which registers pips with 2 decimal place, that is 0.01.

Pip Value

So, hypothetically speaking, let's say you have the USD/GBP currency pair and you get a quote 0.7754. this means 1 USD will get you 0.7754 GBP. A one pip increase - 0.7755 - would mean that 1 USD will then become more valuable as it will earn you a bit more GBPs.

If, say, you then decide to buy 2000 GBPs with US Dollars, you will then first divide the USD/GBP exchange rate then multiply by the number of Euros you want to buy.

So, it will be [1/0.7754] x 2000 = 2579.31. the price paid will be 2579.31.

If there is a one pip increase in the exchange rate - to 0.7755 - then the calculation would be
[1/0.7755] x 2000 = 2578.98.

Therefore, the pip value between the currencies would be 2579.31 - 2578.98 = USD 0.33.

The more one puts in the trading, the higher the pip value.

Pipettes; A Further Figure

Further down the figures, we get the pipette. Pipettes allow spreading to happen over an even wider area, meaning that it further reduces the risks that come with Forex trading. This is measured as $1/10^{th}$ of a pip. In most normal pair currencies, it is measured as the fifth number after the decimal place, but when it comes to the Japanese Yen against the dollar, it is represented as third decimal place. Usually, it is displayed in superscript format.

For example, in 1 USD = 0.77576 GBP, the 6 at the end is the pipette.

Pips and Profits: What Affects Your Gains/Losses?

As stated above, the movement of the currency pair determines whether you make gains or losses.

So, for example, if you want to buy into the USD/EUR pair. If the prices of the Euro goes up when you sell, you profit from the increase. So, say you bought Euros for 1.1843 and then, when you sell, the market price is at 1.1896, your profit will be the 53 pips on the trade.

Relatively speaking, the difference is small. But the Forex market is a big deal, often determining economies of entire countries and the market prices. Gains and losses add up quickly, thus, meaning that the slightest change can have a high impact and have far-reaching consequences. Small changes will often result in small fluctuations which, when considered over time and consistently, will have bigger consequences. Thus, while it may be a small figure to the untrained eye, a seasoned trader knows the value of a pip. Therefore, so should you.

Why Is It Important To Understand Pip

Understanding pips and pip values are important before you put your money into Forex trading. Among the benefits are;

To Follow the Gains/losses

Seasoned traders often gain the advantage by knowing how the fluctuations of pip values will influence their profit/losses.

Understanding the change in pip value helps you as a trader strategies on which deals will be worth putting your stakes.

To Identify Strong Currency Pairs

When you understand the pip values, you will better be able to access the currency pairs in the market, follow through those that combine well and trade favorably and thus, know where to place your risks.

As we have learned above, a small pip change can have wide implications and this could quickly add up to either gains or losses. Therefore, you will have an understanding of this when you look at the currency pairs.

Leverage

Leverage provides you with the ability to trade with amounts of money that are more than you have on your deposits. If the leverage is, say 30, this will mean that, for every one dollar you have in your deposit, for example, you will control 30 in the Forex market, thus, increasing chances of a huge profit.

Therefore, understanding the pip values will allow you better gauge the risks that are involved in the trading you are about to undertake and choose reasonable leverage sizes that won't dent your pockets in the event of losses.

Factors That Determine Pip Value

There are several factors that will determine the pip value;
The currency pairs you chose to trade-in
The size of the transaction
The exchange rate.

However, other factors that will determine the pip spread will be the volatility, uncertainty, and liquidity of the market.

Volatility will often include events that will shift market forces, such as central bank policies. These will often cause the pip spread to increase. In the other end, market volatility refers to the state of the market in the economy. Uncertainty may be caused by political turmoil, as well as events such as elections. In the event of political turmoil, traders will most likely not want to sell due to the sudden spread of pips, meaning that the prices will fluctuate greatly. But this often returns to normal levels once the events have passed.

So, we have learned about what pips are; defined what they mean and their importance to the Forex investor. The pip is the smallest change in value in currency pair trading and is usually represented by the fourth figure in the decimal place, with an exception of the Japanese Yen, which is represented by the third decimal place.

We have also learned how pips are important and the terms that you will come across in relation to the Forex market. We have also learned that the pip value is the 1/10000 of the buying currency (usually the USD) multiplied by the exchange rate. Understanding pip value is important and there are factors that determine the changes in pip values, some of which include the political situation in the given economy.

A smaller fraction still, the pipette, is calculated as $1/10^{th}$ of the pip and is often represented as a superscript in the quote panel after the pip figure.

Chapter 6: How to Read Trading Charts

A trading chart is a sequence of prices of a particular stock over a specified period in the stock market. Unlike before, up to date charts are found online. You can access them using a smartphone, tablet, iPad, laptop or desktop. They are simple at your disposal whenever you need them. The structure of a trading chart is quite simple. It has a y-axis and an x-axis. The y-axis indicates prices of securities while the x-axis indicates time intervals for the period of the chart. The prices run from left to right across the horizontal axis with figures in the farthest right indicating most recent prices. Trading charts are prepared and interpreted by specialists in the stock market who identify, analyze securities and predict their future prices within a specific period. However, you don't have to be a technical analyst to be able to read them as they are quite simple to interpret.

Prices of securities are affected by economic and non-economic factors while the chart's time frame is determined by the amount of data available for a given stock and the ease with which that data can be compressed. Time intervals can be in minutes or hours depending on the period the chart is focusing on. The data in the chart changes from time to time as new buying and selling orders enter the market while old ones are canceled and filled. There are vital data and price points found at the top of the chart. This data gives information about that particular chart, you must know what this identification data means.

Company name

This is the entity, a company or fund whose prices are being analyzed and shown in the chart.

Ticker Symbol

This is a symbol representing the company or fund being traded at that particular time.

Bid

This is normally represented by **B**. It is the highest price a buyer is willing to buy a particular security.

Time Interval

This indicates the time the chart represents. It can be in minutes or hours.

Ask

This is represented by **A**. It indicates the lowest price a seller is willing to sell their security.

Volume

It is represented by **V** on the chart. This is the total number of shares being traded by the stock market in a particular season.

Last

This is the last price quoted for a certain security.

Open

It is represented by **O**. This is the price for which the stock market has opened that day.

Previous Close

This is represented by **PC**. It is the last closing price of the stock the previous day.

High

It is represented as **Hi**. This is the highest price a stock has traded on that day.

Low

Represented as **Lo**, this is the lowest price a stock has traded on that day.

Net CHG

This represents a change in price between the closing price of the previous day and the opening price for the next day. Net % CHG is that change expressed as a percentage of the total price of a particular stock.

Trading charts are classified according to the time frame they represent. These charts can be intraday, daily, weekly and monthly charts. Intraday and daily charts are used by short-term traders and investors in the stock markets. These charts illustrate the prices of stocks within various hours of the day. Weekly charts are used by those traders and investors wishing to analyze intermediate stock prices within the week. Monthly charts are designed for long-term investors and traders. They represent up to years of data for a particular stock market.

Trading charts are represented in the following ways:
- Bar charts
- Line charts
- Candlestick charts

Bar charts are the most complex among the three as they show highs and lows in addition to opening and closing prices. Line graphs have a line drawn from one closing price to another closing price. Candlesticks are the most commonly used because they're easy to read and interpret, they're nothing short of visual aids. Let us look at how these three charts are read and interpreted.

Chart Analysis

To guide you on how to correctly read and interpret a trading chart, we are going to use a sample bar chart, a real one for that matter. The chart we are going to use is that of Weatherford International, whose stocks trade in the New York Securities

Exchange. The period in question is 14th September 2005 at 4.00p

There are four main stages in a stocks bar chart, namely:

- Consolidation

- Uptrend

- Another consolidation

- Downtrend

The chart above broke out of its consolidation in July and assumed an uptrend. A stock is said to be in an uptrend if it is moving forward towards the upper right corner as is the case in our sample chart. This first pullback is the best time for an investor to buy stocks otherwise they'll have to wait for the next trend. The trends then change drastically after a certain period (end of July in our case) marking the beginning of the second pullback. You can still buy stocks at this stage but it is unlikely that that particular trend will last long. If a stock does not maintain its uptrend, it gets into another consolidation before it starts falling. This continuous fall is referred to as the downtrend. The chart above can be predicted to maintain an uptrend and this makes it worth investing in, but before we arrive at this conclusion, we need to look at the finer details in the chart.

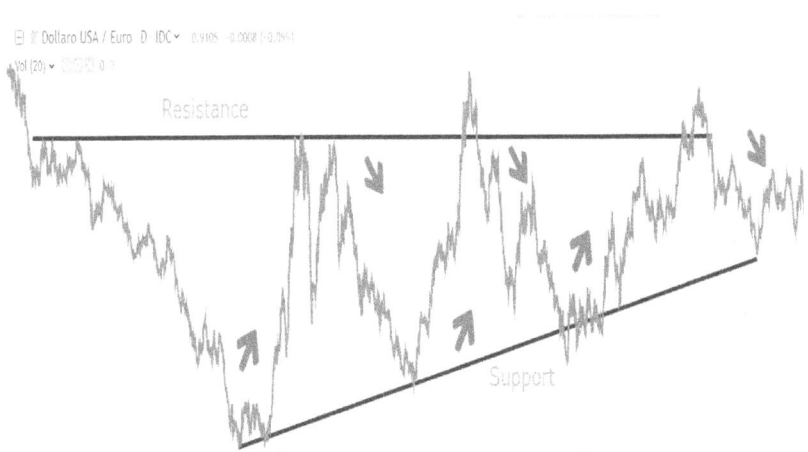

Interpreting Candlesticks

The first thing you need to look at is the price of the stock during a particular period. In our chart, various prices are represented by candlesticks in red, black and white. As the name suggests, these candlesticks are vertical rectangles with a wick extending at its top and bottom. The wick at the top represents a high while the one at the bottom represents a low. Remember the definition of these terms. The nature of the candlesticks will guide you in determining whether you're dealing with a bull market or a bear market. It will also help you study trends in the chart and make accurate predictions about future prices.

- White candles normally represent a bullish market where prices open near the low and close near the high of the period.
- Black candles are quite the opposite of white ones, they represent a bear market where prices open near the high and close near the low.
- A candlestick with a small body and long wick represents a hammer. A hammer is a pattern in the bull market that indicates an uptrend or downtrend (hanging man).
- A pricing line occurs where a long bear candle is followed by a long bull candle that opens slightly below a bear's low.
- A bullish engulfing line occurs when a small bear candle is engulfed by a bigger bull candle after a major downtrend.
- Doji and morning stars are bull market patterns that indicate indecision and imminent fall respectively.

- Spinning tops occur when the distance between open and close and that between low and high are negligible. It is an indication that the pattern is neutral.
- When smaller candles overlap on the body of a bigger candle, it causes a Harami pattern. This pattern indicates a loss of interest in a certain stock.

Smoothness

The next thing after the price that we need to look out for in this chart is its smoothness. If its trend is smooth like in our sample chart, it means that the stock is reliable and the investor is free to invest in it with confidence. A chart that is not smooth should be a red light about the behavior of that stock. You can't give a guarantee that the stocks will go up in the future.

Breakout

As a trader or investor, a breakout is another feature you must look out for while analyzing a stock chart. Breakouts happen immediately after the opening bells ring, in the middle or towards the end of the trading period. Always aim to buy a pullback as close to the breakout as possible as this is the best time to measure the level interest of a particular stock. It will put you a step ahead of someone that buys later. Traders use breakouts to decide whether to buy more of a certain stock in the future or not to buy.

Range

Moving forward, a stock that is assumed to do well in the future has a relatively wide range of candlesticks across it. A small range means that the stock is progressing in an uptrend but is struggling. Such a stock does not guarantee 100 percent safety and thus should be approached with caution.

Patterns

Patterns in the chart are something you also need to look out for though not very significant. As long as the pattern is moving up, its shape does not matter. The pattern comes in handy when we're confronted with two stocks with almost similar patterns. Always choose the one pattern you can interpret without much difficulty.

Gaps

Some stocks will exhibit gaps along the time horizon. As much as these gaps are normal, look out for abnormally many gaps in a chart as this may mean that a stock has had too many buyers already. Many gaps in a chart is an indication that many breakouts have occurred, a time when many pullbacks are bought. Investing in that kind of stock is a major gamble with two extreme outcomes. It could be a huge gain or a painful loss.

Fibonacci retracement levels

These are levels that indicate the weakness of a particular stock. A stock is considered safe if its Fibonacci retracement level is above 50%. Any level below that means that the stock is doomed and might collapse any time. Avoid investing in stocks with degenerating prices.

Tails and Shadows

These are features at the bottom of the candlesticks that indicate that the stock is getting support from financially powerful individuals and institutions. It means that you are insulated from a possible fall within that trading period. This kind of support is represented by red or green lines running below the candlesticks. A stock that gets support will jump to its previous high, thus maintaining an upward trend. From our sample graph, this trend can be seen between August and September sixth.

Volume

As mentioned earlier, the volume is the total number of shares trading in a given period. A stock that has a bigger volume is doing well and many people are interested in it. Although this is a good stock to invest in, it can also turn out to be a risky investment. Too much interest in a particular stock may lead to it being overbought. Its prices will likely fall in this case. Stocks with a low volume pullback, on the other hand, are considered to be struggling. They are still worth investing in but with a lot of moderation. Every next one of its breakouts could be the last unless institutional investors come to its rescue.

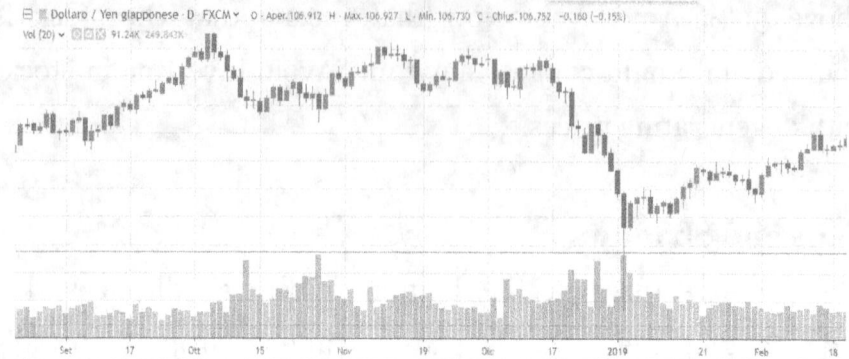

Having gone through all the basics and details about trading charts, it is now time for you to familiarize yourself with as many of them as possible and interpret them accordingly. These terms and features might look scary at first but trust me, they will be second nature every next time you interact with each. You should be flexible enough to realize that the thousands of new charts you meet every day require the exact approach like this one so you shouldn't be intimidated. After a while, you will be able to prepare your charts which will be much easier to interpret compared to those that have been prepared by someone else. Lastly, keep in mind that nothing is ever certain in the stock market even with a correct analysis of the charts. The unpredictability might be caused by external factors like government policies that might come sweeping through the market like a tsunami, catching everyone unawares and causing chaos.

Chapter 7: Comparison between Fundamental and Technical Analysis

As a trader, you can be confused about whether to opt for a technical or analysis. But, it doesn't matter. as long as you learn the best time to enter or exit a trade, you can choose one or a combination of these analyses. But, before choosing any, you need to understand how both work and if they will assist you in making good trading decisions.

Fundamental analysis requires economic and statistical data too. Also, it uses data to determine currency strength. On the other hand, technical analysis use chat patterns to forecast price movements. Like flags and triangles.

Well, read on to get insights on the similarities and differences between fundamental and technical analysis.

What is the fundamental analysis?

Fundamental analysis looks at the market an interesting perspective. It analyses social, political, and economic factors that may affect the demand and supply of an asset. Fundamental analysis strives to find out the actual value of an asset, give a comparison to the current price, and also locate a trading opportunity. In the Forex world, supply and demand determine the currency exchange rate. Also, it aims to look at different factors which determine the country's economy is doing well or is facing an economic crisis. Lastly, it analyses the financial market with the aim of predicting future prices.

Price of an asset can differ from time to time sometimes the markets May under-price, misprice, or overprice an asset. But, later, the market often normalizes price. These are fundamental analysis.

A stable economy strengthens the country's currency and vice versa. To obtain a country currency, then one has to purchase its asset. Well, foreign investors, business people usually invest in a country to get access to their currency.

When a country economy improves, then, their dollar is most likely to gain strength. Fundamental analysis often tends to predict a projection on business performance. Investors use a broader spectrum of the stock market to evaluate the review of economic factors like it's strength and specific market conditions.

Also, it evaluates show to manage and make business decisions and also determine credit risk. Valuate a stock and predict when the price will evolve.

Factors that are affect countries economics

Several factors contribute to the decline or incline of a countries economy. They include:

- Unemployment rates
- Monetary policy
- Housing stats
- International trade a
- Manufacturing

Fundamental factors that influence currency movement

Economic indicators

An economic indicator is a piece of detailed information about the country financial status. It's released by the government or an organization. The results are released at particular scheduled times that are: weekly, monthly, or even quarterly.

The information released can lead to higher returns in the financial markets. With the data, one can determine whether a countries economy has improved, is stagnant or has decreased. The commotion can occur when prices are released before the release of official rates. This condition is known as "priced market."

When reports are released, traders usually check on the weakness and strength in the various economies before venturing into a trade. The following are economic indicators you should watch out.

Interest rates

Interest rates have an impact on the unemployment rate, investment trade production, and inflation. There is a different kind of interest rates; central banks around the world usually offer loan to banks, business, and citizens of a country. Sometimes the central bank can decide to lower the interest's rates so to stabilize an economy.

But, when the interest's rates are too low, and lots of loans are issued, then it's likely to taint lousy image on the economy. That's why they sometimes regulate by raising it.

Interest rates are an excellent place to look for trading opportunities. They tend to control economies growth. High-interest rates make financial assets attractive, thus luring more investors to invest, and the result, is the currency value increases.

Inflation

Inflation is the prices of goods in a period over time. The government and the central banks work to enhance the balance. When the inflations rates are high, then the value of the currency is likely to depreciate

Most developed countries believe that moderate inflation signifies a growing economy in developed nations. On the other hand, developing nations believe that a decreased or maintain inflation is excellent as it keeps the country economy check.

Gross domestic products (GDP)

GDP contains a total market of value of goods and services produced in the country yearly. GDP Increases in an unhealthy for the particular nation

Industrial production

Usually, shows the productivity of factories, mines industries, and utilities in a nation. Traders who use the utility industry before deciding to trade can be significantly affected by the changes in weather. Weather sometimes causes volatility to the currency of a particular nation.

When you chose fundamental analysis, you should consider the following factors to maximize your results.

- Have an economic calendar- in your calendar; you can list indicators as well as look into the future market.
- Check what's trending on the economic market- you should keep up with the information the economic news and watch out the news that could be a threat to your trade and vice versa.

- Give it time- don't react immediately to the news released. Take your time as rush decisions may hurt your trade. Numbers usually get changed, and sometimes they are revised. The more patient you are, the more good choices you are likely to make.

- Understand the market expectations of particular data. Check if the expectations of a requirement are met. The information is more useful than the data provided.

Tools for fundamental analysis

You need to understand the depths of fundamentals analysis. The knowledge of the key ratios will help you follow stocks more accurately and carefully. Most fundamental tools focus on growth, earning, and the value that is in the market.

Price to earnings ratio (P/E) - this ratio shows a comparison of current sales of a market stock and their share per earnings.

Earnings per share (EPS) - investigates what percentages of profit the company stock assigns

Dividend yield- usually expressed as a percentage. Paid in a yearly period and lastly, it compares to the annual shared price.

Price to sale ratio (P/R-) compares company stalk to the revenues.

Projected earnings growth (PEG)- analyses a year's growth of a stock

Price to book ratio (P/B) – also known as the price to equity ratio. You can determine this ratio when determine by diving a closing the stock most present closing price and the value of the last quarter of the book to the cost per share.

The price to book ratio - the price to book ratio shows asset value as it appears in the company books.

Return on equity_ to get a return on equity; you divide shareholder equity with the company's net income.

Advantages of fundamental analysis

Uses analytical data- the results ensures that there is no bias. The results found are sound financial data making it concrete to use.

Easy to understand- the accounting financial analysis will help you understand better how the market works

There is a focus- fundamental analysis not only focus one, but several long term elements like demographics, economics, technology, and consumer trends to get the desired results.

Use a systematic approaching to get values- the analytical and statistical tools you use enables you to choose whether to buy or sell in a trade.

Disadvantages

Takes a lot of time- to get accurate results, you have to dig into various economic indicators. Usually, it not only takes time but you need to be willing to work hard and obtain the results that you need.

Lots of assumptions involved- there is a lot of assumptions involved in forecasting financials, you should expect the best, and the worst scenarios as unexpected politic and economic change can result in problems.

Technical analysis

Technical analysis is a theoretical framework used by Forex traders to study price movement. A trader can consider a historical price movement. You study the price pattern of a particular specific asset. Additionally, you use indicators, technical studies, and other analysis tools before embarking on a trade. You should check what happens and make a potential price movement. Charts are easy to visualize; you can see clearly how the market is fairing on. Additionally, you can view past data, current trends, and predicts what the future would be like.

Chart watching basics you should know;

Moving averages
Helps tin determine the overall trading. A trend condition usually, it plots the average price of a security in a particular period.

Price trends
Checks I stock price are accelerating or decelerating. And the amount of time and the period in which the price has stayed his way. Most chartists buy a security that is up in the trends.

Volume
Volume acts as lie detectors. With volume, one can predict how strong a trend influence may be. Decreasing volume indicates that a trend can be on the verge of a reversal.

Appear above or below a chart.
All the information on a current market is reflected on a price. When you know the history of the trading market, you will be

able to make great trading decisions. It acts as a map, guiding you on how to curate or conduct a trade.

Technical analysis was self-fulfilling as it's subjective. Technicians use various methods to study the price patterns. That is;

Technical analysis candle- candle patterns show high, low, open, and close levels. With this, you can get clues on how the buyers and sellers reacted during the previous years.

Technical analysis chart - the chart gives clarity to buyers and sellers throughout the market.

Technical analysis indicators- using this chart as trade will help you understand the market conditions. You will also view the rising and the falling momentums of the market

Importance of a Technical Analysis

There are many uncertainties in this market. But as a trader, you have to take a risk and work on probabilities. As much as the market can be chaotic, you will identify patterns and make the most out of it. With a clear review of the charts, and study of the market, you have the potential of making the correct choices when it comes to your trade. You will know when to enter a market. And, the most important thing is, you learn how to get out of a trade and when.

Secondly, you learn to identify patterns mark can figure out what to do when particular issues arise in the market.

Also, you get to learn to determine the probabilities and jump into the right opportunities, when odds work on your favor.

How do you conduct a technical analysis?

Determine which security interests you -For instance, you can do research on which sector is at the moment trading this will assist in deciding on what to buy or sell

Choose a strategy that suits you -each stock is unique. And each cannot utilize the same approach.

Choose a trading account. To maximize profits, go for the account with the right functionality, cost, and also support.

Comprehend your tools -Knowing thee tools that fit your trading strategies and tools is essential. Free tools are available for you to learn and understand the features.
Try out to test your system with the market data before jumping on the bandwagon of trading. Choose a few indicators

that can fit the technical indicator requirements you chose. Monitor how they perform each day.

Advantages of technical analysis

You learn when to exist and enter a trade- through the patterns in charts; you will learn how to jump out of a trade.

They provide you with the right information directions are essential to in any field. Technical analysis offers precisely what you need to navigate this industry.

Get information on the current trends- prices tend to increase or decrease. Usually, they reflect on the information of an existing asset to make decisions.

Differences between fundamental and technical analysis

As much as the two analysis help you get trading results. They have numerous differences. Some are here below

1. Fundamental analysis uses economic m reports of industry statistics and news events to analyze data and make predictions; also, it forecasts share prices on the basis company statics and economic industry. Technical analysis uses a chart to analyze data and majorly focuses on internal data and market statistics.

2. Fundamental analysis is concerned with the investments. The investors usually hold or buy a stock of a company with the information got. Technical analysis is more concerned with the trade.

3. The security of the future prices us determine by the past and present performance a company make in Forex trading, while indicators and charts are the ones that determine the future market prices

4. A long term trader usually utilizes fundament analysis. Long term investors buy stocks containing enormous dividends pay-out and regularly release or sell them after several years when the stocks have passed through several fluctuations while short berm traders usually utilize technical analysis. Such traders o did not buy or keep goods for years, but instead, they focus more on short term profits.

5. Fundamental utilizes the intrinsic value of stock got when one analyses income statements like cash flow management, profit margins, and returns on equity. They predict the future of the market. A technical analysis, depend on a chart, technical indicators, resistance, and support to analyze future trend patterns.

6. In fundamental analysis, no assumptions are made while assumptions like similar price trends are not news, in technical analysis

7. Fundamentals analysts don't need to go back to history to find to discover past prices and the fluctuations

incurred. However, technicians trades re-occur, and the possibility of history repeating itself is high.

So which analysis techniques should you choose?

Most analysis on street walls prefers fundamental analysis to technical analysis. Both technical and fundamental have their advantages and disadvantages. But a good investor will point out that their combination of both the two, end up producing t exceptional results.

Risk management

Knowledge of both fundamental and technical approach can help to handle any risk involved in a trade. Economic can tell if the attitude of particular market changes, but fails to inform you when the view of the market is wrong. Technical analysis helps you manage risk as you can view on the charts and can help you revise a market view.

Also, a combination of the two analyses can confirm specific trends. When, most people in a country expect a higher interest rate, but it doesn't manifest, then that countries' currency would likely decrease in value. Furthermore, When the currency continues rising, there could be a possibility of other factors involved rather than the interest rate. A technical trader can use the way markets reacts to fundamental news to their advantage

Partying shots

When marketers try to focus on future price movements, they use fundamental analysis to look at issues such as political developments and economic data.; they use technical analysis to read charts and interpret price movements or instead come the two. That what, you need to do a trader.

Chapter 8: Tools, Indicators, and Patterns of Trading

Tools of trade

This is a term used to help a person decide the kind of property they should use to earn and make a living. According to bankruptcy law, the exemption for tools of the trade is usually determined by the state in the state exemption statutes. The exemption can also be determined by federal law in the federal bankruptcy exemptions. The period of time in which a person lived in a state before filing could also be a determinant of the exemption. Lawyers assist their clients to understand which properties are exempt and the exemptions apply.

Anything a person can prove they use as a tool for trade is marked as a separate exemption from assets they own. This means that a person can be allowed an exemption for households separately from assets they use to make a living. One person may provide their vehicle as a property they own while another may produce their vehicle as a taxi which earns him his daily bread.

Having the right tools for trading will guarantee success for anyone starting. An experienced trader may not really be concerned about the tools they use but for beginners, the tools count.

Examples of Tools Used For Trade.

- Light speed financial broker – here a broker or a group of brokers breaks into different groups of specialization. The specialization is determined by the services they offer and the financial instrument used. The options for these brokers are Forex, stocks, long term investing and scalping brokers. Light speed brokers are very convenient for day time traders because of their direct accessibility and fast executions.

- Trade ideas stock scanning software – after establishing a good broker, the next step is finding the stock to trade with. The ability to determine stocks before they make a big move is what determines a more profitable trader. Trade ideas software helps in stock scanning for volume spikes, HOD movers to establish the gainers and the losers and things like that. This is the best software there is that scans the market and finds the winning stocks.

- signal charting – the third step is getting high-quality charts. The broker you chose makes come his standard charts. Those will work for you for some time until you decide to use ones that allow you to draw and write formulas. Signal allows one to run charts on 8 monitors without time delay. This is advantageous to people who like observing several stocks at once. it also allows installation of custom scripts. Custom scripts can be used as custom indicators for reversals and drawing support and resistance lines.

- Breaking news provider – every morning, a trader should start by reviewing the market. After the review, you look at the catalyst to determine why stocks are moving higher. Reasons for the stocks could be moving up in consideration to the market, or a strong sector while other times it may be a unique catalyst like earnings. Breaking news provide the headlines for when the stocks are spiking.

- TAS market profile – this software is best in helping make trade decisions. It has several tools in it. Among them is a TAS scanner which allows one to observe stocks moving at different timings with different levels of buying and selling.

Having the right tool may not guarantee success in the trading world but it will give the right directions that will help make trading easier. The right tool will also provide an advantage for a trader over other traders who do not have the tools.

Indicators of Trade

This is a measure or gauge of trade that allows analyzing of prices and provides trade signals. Indicators provide trade signals that alert a trader when it is time to trade. Day trading indicators are not to be used as the only plan. They should be used along with a well laid out though to make it a useful trading tool. No matter the kind of trade one is involved in, having many trading indicators may bring inconsistency with trading decisions due to the complexities involved. Keeping it simple could simply be the trick to making clear and less stressful trading decisions.

Trading indicators should not, therefore, be taken as the only method relied on trading. However, using indicators alongside other trading variables may come in handy. Getting rid of the many indicators helps traders have a simplistic approach to the market.

Role of Technical Indicators

- Get the direction trend

- Determine the momentum or lack of momentum in the market

- Determine if and if not the market is growing

- Get the volume to determine how popular a market is with traders

Getting the same type of indicators that on the chart that give the same information is where the issue is. This is because you may give conflicting information or get more information than you may be stressful. The main shortcoming of most indicators is that since they are gotten from price, they delay the price. There are rules that one can use to determine useful indicators for day trading, swing trading, and position trading. This include among others:

Choosing one trend indicator such as moving average and one momentum trading indicator is the simplest rule.

Knowing well the perimeters you want to investigate before you decide on the trading indicators which you will use on your charts. Then know well the indicator you chose in terms of how it works, calculations it does and the effects it will bring for your trading decisions.

Indicators work only depending on how they are incorporated into the trading plan. Some indicators like MACD and CCI are best at calculating information. Others like alligator indicator are fast at showing a market that is trending and ranging. Other indicators will show directions and act as entry and exit signals of trade. The usage of a basic indicator along with a well laid out trading plan by back, forward and demo can you put you ahead of trade with many complicated indicators. Netpicks offers systems that test trade plans, prove trading systems and trading indicators.

Threat of Optimization

There is a hindrance or barriers for when one is searching for trading indicators that work for one's style and trading plan. Most systems sell standard indicators that are fine-tuned to show successful results from the past. This is a disadvantage since it does not take into account the market changes. Using the standard settings for all indicators help avoid over-optimization trap which helps a trader not to focus on today's market progress and miss on the future.

Best Technical Trading Indicators

For day trading, a trader should test several indicators individually then later as a combination. One may end up with say 3-5 good ones that are evergreen and decide to switch off depending on the market at that particular day or the asset trading.

Regardless of the type of trade, day, Forex or futures the idea is to keep it simple with the indicators. Use one indicator per category to avoid repeating the same thing and distraction.

Combining Indicators

Combining pairs of indicators on the price chart helps to identify points to initiate trade. A good example is a combination of RSI and moving average convergence which combined suggest and reinforce a trading signal. When choosing sets it's important to find one indicator considered a leading indicator and another that is a lagging indicator.

Leading indicators show signals before the forms for entering trade has been made. Lagging indicators on the other hand show signals after the formation have happened. Therefore lagging indicators can confirm leading indicators and help a trader from trading on wrong signals.

Choosing a combination of pairs that include indicators of different types instead of the same type is highly advisable. It does not make sense to observe a combination of the same type of indicators because they will still give the same information.

Multiple Indicators

Using multiple indicators boosts trading signals and may increase chances of telling out false signals.

Refining Indicators

It is important for a trader to take note and record the performance of the indicators they are using. Knowing the weaknesses of an indicator to determine if it gives a lot of false signals, if sometimes it fails to signal or if it signals too late or too early is essential. Knowing these things about the indicator will help determine what the indicator is best suited for. You may find that the indicator is suited for Forex instead of stocks while you thought it was just ineffective. This might help you decide if you want to trade the indicator for another or to just simply change how it's calculated. Doing this refining, will help an indicator work best for you, and also for you to find the best indicator for different types of trading.

Patterns of Trade

This is generally how trade takes place. It is the movement of price against a specific period of time. Patterns of trade are made of charts drawn in lines to connect proportional prices like the closing dates for a number of days.

Hammer Patterns

This is a reversal candlestick pattern that happens at the bottom of the depression. It is created when the open, high, and close prices are about the same price and a lower long shadow twice the length of the main body happens. In other words, hammer candlesticks form when shares fall from the opening prices due to pressure caused in selling. But then they manage to cover most losses experienced within the trading period.

Even when a hammer pattern is a single candle, an observation of the surrounding candles within that single stick is needed to confirm if it is indeed a hammer candlestick pattern.

If the hammer candlestick pattern forms in a depression, it is regarded as a market depression or support.

Verification Signals

- When the candle has a long lower shadow, there is a high chance of price reversal.

- When there is a lot of trade volume the day the hammer forms, it probably means a blow off in the trade.

- When the candle has a gap from the previous day closing price, it means that a strong reversal is expected to happen because the price opened higher a day after the hammer.

- A green candle will show the sign of a bull while a red sign will show the sign of a bear.

The Inverted Hammer Pattern

This candlestick is formed after depression and is a sign of a trend reversal. It looks like the reverse of a hammer candlestick pattern and its formation indicates an uptrend called a shooting star. If there is a downtrend and an inverted hammer with the sign of a bull is formed, it means that the prices delayed the upward move by a high increase during the day. Then the sellers made the prices push back near the open. Prices having increased show the bulls trying to overpower the bears. The next day determines if the prices go higher or lower and their observation is very important. The bullish pattern is a continuous pattern that represents a fall in the market after a strong unexpected move. The bullish pattern does not necessarily require the use of an indicator because it is itself a price action.

The bullish flag pattern is a strong technical pattern in that it has the ability to form in the shortest time frame of a minute up to a whole monthly chart. This pattern is constructed in two sections; the first is a powerful sustained rally while the other one is that, it has a tight range that is contained in two parallel lines.

There has been an immense growth in the global economy over the years. This has resulted in a change in the pattern trade. The changes include deindustrialization, the participation of communist countries and the emergence of India and China.

Although growth has been affected by short term changes due to the economic cycle, the value of trade has immensely improved. Globalization is taking over. Trade openness has also increased in most countries as an effect of globalization.

Chapter 9: Risk Management and Trading Psychology

Risk management generally refers to identifying, evaluating, and prioritizing risks. It involves coordinating and economically applying resources to ensure minimization, monitoring, and controlling the uncertainty of unfortunate events leading to maximization of profit.

On the other hand, trading psychology focuses on emotions and mental state of an individual that predicts the trading succession or failure. It is the most effective aspect of trading as it touches directly on the behavior of traders from day to day hence helping in the forecasting of the end result of this particular activity.

Risk Management and Trading Psychology work hand in hand in improving performance on a trader in the Forex market. The understanding of both concepts enables the trader to understand and accept the trends in the market and adjust with them appropriately. These concepts help the traders in coming up with good trading plans and strategies that attract maximum profit.

In this chapter, we are going to discuss the various risks involved in Forex trading and the psychological aspect of trading.

Below are various risks that apply to Forex trading and the possible management practices that traders can apply to avoid unnecessary losses.

Political Risk

Every country has its own time of carrying out elections and country politics vary in all countries. Effects of politics in one country may affect trade in that country incurring a loss in trading. The political instability that sometimes arises during elections may have a great influence on the country's exchange rate imposing severe loss on the Forex market.

Traders can manage this type of risk by maintaining a diversified portfolio and this is only possible if they understand that this risk is worth taking. They should also monitor the investments for likely political risks. Risk monitoring and maintenance play a big role in reducing the severe effects of risk upon occurrence.

Interest Rate Risk

Interest Rate Risk is normally experienced when there's fluctuation in the interest rates. Most companies always give out loans with the aim of earning themselves an interest when the loan is paid back. It is the role of banks in the countries to decide the interest rates on credits. When the commercial bank in a country lowers their interest rate, it will definitely affect traders who had already given out loans expecting a higher interest rate.

Interest Rate Risk in the Forex market can be managed by categorizing the mismatches depending on the dates of their maturity. These categories can be placed in up to 6 months or the previous 6 months. The environment of interest rate should be analyzed continuously to predict changes that influence the outstanding intermissions.

Risk of Ruin

Risk Of Ruin financially relates to the possibility of losing all the capital one has invested in a business. In the Forex market, the probability of losing your investment capital is so high for beginners or those that easily give up and let go. This type of risk is the most common in Forex trading. When you wrongly predict price fluctuation, you may find yourself losing twice as much as you are gaining.

This type of risk can be reduced when the traders effectively calculate the possibility of loss or gain occurring, upon which one can prefer to avoid the risk in case the probability of loss becomes higher than the probability of gain. However, avoiding the risk will force the trade to think of a different way of investing since they will have foregone the previous one.

Transactional Risk

Transaction risk mentions the adverse impact of fluctuation on the foreign exchange rate on a completed transaction previous to settlement.Transaction risk in most cases increases with the increase in time between starting a contract and resolving the contract.

The best possible way of managing transaction risk is by improving liquidity control and management. Other effective ways of handling transaction risk include;

- Surveillance by a board of administrators
- Sufficient risk management strategies and processes
- A specific structure for describing country submissions
- An appropriate procedure for inspecting country risk
- Having a rating structure for country risk
- Initiated country subjection limits
- Continuous evaluation of country terms
- Time-based strain testing of foreign submissions
- Sufficient internal evaluation and an assessment task

Credit Risk

Credit Risk refers to the uncertainty of receiving an outstanding currency position as earlier agreed. This is usually a result of actions taken by the counterparty willingly or unwillingly. The organizations that are commonly attached to this type of risk are banks and corporations. Private companies and individual traders rarely experience credit risk.

Credit Risk can be managed by;

- Thoroughly checking the credit records of a new customer.

- Using the immediate sale to start developing a relationship with the customer.

- Establishing limits of credit offered to the customer.

- Making sure that the agreement for your sale's credit terms is very clear.

- Having credit risk insurance.

Settlement Risk

This is a type of risk that is usually caused by the variance in time zones from one continent to another, which causes a difference in the prices of currency trade at different times on the same day of trading. Whenever this happens, some parties may be forced to declare insolvency affecting payment since the party that has been declared insolvent or declared insolvency has to be paid, antecedent to the execution of own payment by the party.

In this case, it is the duty of the bank to find a way of reducing the loss. The bank has to come up with a balanced approach to ensure that it won't experience huge loss by paying the counterparties. The bank can decide to reduce its limit with the concerned counterparty or to suspend the issuing of payment instructions regarding the remaining deals with the counterparty in order to protect it.

Replacement Risk

Replacement risk is a type of risk that occurs when a bank fails. The failure of the bank affects the counterparties of the particular bank with the fear that they might not receive the funds that should be allocated to them from the bank that had failed. Replacement risk is one of the feared risks that a trader can experience. However, this type of risk can still be managed by traders who are widely exposed to the trading of currency. It might be hard for beginners even though some beginners after conducting relevant research always turn out to act like PRO.

To manage this type of risk, you first need to identify the current risk position of the company. You need to how exposed you are to this kind of risk and how the company has been handling it in case of occurrence. This will help you in planning and budgeting for the risk to avoid its severity.

Country Risk

Country risk refers to the risk that a foreign government backtracks on its financial agreements. The reason as to why most countries backtrack their financial commitments and bonds is because of political instability which creates insecurities in the business sector. The emergence of country risk in one country affects other countries that are involved making it hard to trade with the country.

Marginal Risk

Marginal Risk is a type of risk that an issuer assumes in a contract in foreign trading. It always becomes a debt when the investor defaults. Marginal risk is sometimes associated with weather that affects trading in affected countries changing the exchange rates.

The most appropriate way of dealing with this type of risk to accept the risk and move on to the next possible mismatch.

Liquidity Risk

This is a type of risk that occurs when a bank is unable to meet its obligations. This adversely affects fired traders who have invested high capital on the market. Liquidity risk negatively affects the bank's stability affecting the interest rate thus low exchange rates.

For a firm to be in able to control liquidity risk, the firm must have adequate analytic capabilities to project the cash flow for all transaction adding to millions.

Other types of risks that are experienced in day to day business include;

- Horizon risk – this type of risk occurs due to shortening of an investment horizon that may press an investor in selling an investment they had planned to hold for a long term. When this occurs when the market price is low then a loss is recorded.

- Concentration Risk – this term describes the potential of risk in a bank's portfolio usually caused by concentration one sector.

- Reinvestment Risk – this occurs upon the canceling of a particular investment forcing the investor to find an alternative way of investing their capital to avoid huge loss. This reduces the expected gains since the investment terms differ from one organization to another.

- Inflation Risk – this is a type of risk that comes up in case of fluctuation of purchasing cost caused by inflation affecting the cash flow.

These types of risks apply everywhere and have different approaches. They LP handled in different ways depending on the level of their severity. These approaches include;

- Risk acceptance – this is where a person decides to accept the risk that they have identified. In this case, nothing is done to reduce the effect of the risk, rather, the outcome and consequences are bared by the concerned party.

- Risk avoidance – here the trader attempts to avoid the impact of the risk by refusing to take the risk. They prefer letting go of the business to taking the identified risk.

- Risk transfer – in this case, a third party is involved. When a trader transfers the risk to someone else, in most cases an insurance company, the person will face the outcomes of risk for them. The trader, therefore, will not be affected by the impact of this particular risk.

- Risk-sharing – this is the practice of muddling the risk to different organizations by taking an insurance cover. In case of an occurrence of the risk, these organizations will participate partially in handling the risk. This reduced the burden of the risk to the person investing.

- Risk maintenance – this involves setting aside maintenance resources that will be used to reduce the effect of the risk upon occurring. The resources are prioritized basically for handling the predicted risk.

- Risk assumption – this is a situation where the investor attempts to ignore the particular risk and assumes it never happened. In this case, nothing is done to reduce the severity of the risk. By assuming the risk, the person puts up with the related impacts through the investment period.

The psychology aspect of trading is also an essential tool in the Forex market. Psychological preparation helps a trader to comply with the market situations and adjust effectively to the changes that affect trading. There are several aspects of psychology that affect trading everywhere. Below are some of the aspects with detailed information on how each affects trading in the Forex market.

Risk-Taking

In-kind of the market, you must always be ready to take risks. Taking risks doesn't mean you are only going to face a loss. Some risks are associated with profit-making and roughly 40-50% risks that are commonly taken by traders have attracted gains. As a trader you must be psychologically prepared to handle risks the way they coming hoping that everything will turn out positively. Avoiding risks isn't the right way of carrying out trade. You might avoid all risks and find yourself not investing any more for the fear of losing. Be the person that try something new but having at the back of your mind that there are a lot of consequences involved.

Discipline

Anyone who wants to invest in any kind of business must attain some level of discipline. Forex trading calls for both financial and emotional discipline. As a trader, you should be in a position to control your emotions in order to succeed in the business world. You must learn to accept the challenges and be able to attack them positively aiming at the better side of it. Someone who is emotionally weak will get upset with everything and will not know how to move forward in case of a disaster that strikes the market trend. Being financially disciplined also helps a trader in making decision on how to invest his/her capital and what to expect.

Fear

Fear is the worst enemy of success. Most people always have the urge to invest in the business but the fear of failing has up to date disabled them from going for what would change their lifestyle and financial status. To become a successful trader, you should not let fear consume you to the extent of not following your heart desires. Always be ready to follow your heart work harder towards achieving your goal. Never give a chance for fear to kill your dream.

Hope

Hope means having a constant feeling that something good is going to happen. Without hope, you can never move forward. When you have an interest in investing in Forex trading, you must be in a state of emotions to believe that what you are doing is worth your struggle and that in the new future you will get to learn how it works and that you will benefit from it as much as really expected. You also need to be emotionally stable so that you don't get affected with the longer it takes to have everything move smoothly.

Greed

Greed is the unending lust for money. Wanting to have more money than you work for. Greed can heavily affect your business if you don't allow your mind to accept that money don't just come by itself but that you have to work hard for it. One thing you have to conceive in mind is that you can never earn more by doing less. Everything takes time to mature and so does money take time to grow.

Patience

Patience is the greatest gift you can offer yourself as a trader. Nothing is done in a hurry ever turns out well. When you allow you to allow yourself to understand that good thing take time, then you are good to go. Do not give up easily on what you have started. Go for what you wanted that pushed you to get start and keep hoping that with time you will achieve your goal. Being impatient usually leads to mental toucher. When you are in a hurry to reach the highest level within the shortest time will only do more harm to your brain. It can even lead to emotional depression.

Regret

Regret is the worst part of investing in a business. Regretting something that you had earlier considered best for you is the worst feeling ever. Yes it is okay to feel bad, it is okay to regret but it is not okay to give up immediately you spot negativity in your business and start regretting the step you had taken.

In order to succeed in the Forex market, you must be in a position to understand all the risks involved and how to manage each of them. You should also prepare psychologically to face the risks involve and know how to balance between your emotions and your business.

Chapter 10: Back Testing

The Back Testing Strategies

Backtesting is a method that is used when an investor is applying the trading strategy into the historical data in order for them to test the accuracy of the strategy in the prediction of the real results. Through backtesting, a trader is able to optimize their trading strategy. One's success in Forex trading is determined by their experience in the Forex trading business. Being in a position to develop a trading strategy will enable you to be able to find the best ways to trade in order for them to trade and get profits.

A trader is required to backtest their trading strategy which will enable them to avoid losing their accounts which may result from choosing a trading strategy that isn't profitable. Backtesting on the trading strategy enables a trader to be able to get a clear picture of how the trading will perform in the available market conditions. Backtesting is all about making the trading strategy work with the former market statistics.

It takes between 10 to 15 years to evaluate the reliability of a trading strategy. This means that it is a continuous process. A trader will keep back testing until they are able to tell that their strategies are a success. It would not be wise to make sure that you take your time to backtest. This is because whenever a trader takes a shorter time, they may succeed in that current

95

market but once the trend changes, they may lose a large part of the trading account. It is therefore important to ensure that one does backtesting for a longer period of time.

Through backtesting, a trader is able to get valuable feedback statistically about the system they are using. Traders are able to get feedback on percentages of the gained and lost net as well as the average percentages gained or lost and also the average bars that were held. The percentage of invested capital which has been invested in the market is also visible as well as the ratios of the wins and losses. A trader is also able to get an analysis in percentages of all the returns made throughout the year. Finally, you will be able to tell the percentage of the risks that will be involved in the production of specific returns.

Every trader should ensure that they remember the below factors when backtesting.

1. Taking current market drifts into consideration when testing a given strategy. This is because market trends keep changing hence the reason for backtesting over a long period of time. This will enable a trader to experience how the strategies work over a period of time.

2. Putting the universe where the backtesting was done into consideration. This will be of great help in ensuring that the trader limits the genre to the targeted strategy.

3. Watching the number of bars held closely. This will help a lot in ensuring that the trader raises the number of

bars which helps in reducing the commission costs and in return improving the trader's overall returns.

4. The trader's exposure. When a trader is exposed, they can either incur losses or improve on their profits. Every trader's aim is to improve their profits. They are therefore encouraged to maintain risks at below 70 % in order to ensure that the risks are minimal. This will enable them to easily transit from different stocks easily.

5. Using an annualized return tool. This is a tool that traders use when benchmarking the systems they are using. The tools give a comparison of the returns they make against any other investments they have. A trader is able to go through all the returns which give a clear picture of the diminished and improved risks.

6. Backtesting over-optimization. A trader should ensure that the results remain relatively the same now and even in the future. This is because there are strategies which may be doing well now but may not do well in the future. The past performance will be a reflection of the results one will get in the future. It is therefore important to ensure that every trader paper trades a given system which they are sure it is tried and tested before implementing it.

Through backtesting, a trader is able to develop a reliable trading system. Traders are able to optimize and make the required improvements to their strategies. This can only happen when a trader ensures that the strategies are effectively interpreted and optimized. There are two types of backtesting that one can use. They include automated backtesting and manual backtesting.

Automated Back Testing

Automated backtesting is referred to as the creation of a program which will automatically and close your trades. The programs include Expert Advisors which normally based on the technical algorithm. Its task is to open and manage your trades whenever there are technical issues. In this type of trading, programs are created while some are purchased. It is an exercise that takes a lot of time which makes it expensive also. This means that it is not favorable for people who may be serious in succeeding in the trading business. It may not be favorable since one does not gain any experience. However, the experience is very vital when it comes to one's growth in business. For this reason, traders who are serious about succeeding in business are advised to avoid automated backtesting and focus on other trading strategies.

Manual Back Testing

Whenever a trader goes through their trading platform from the previous period and forwards from bar to bar using the forward arrow on their keyboard, they are able to evaluate their strategy and see how it's doing in the market. That is what manual backtesting is all about. Traders are able to evaluate and see how the manual backtesting strategy will do in various markets. As they analyze the markets, they are able to see the areas that would need improvement and put extra effort into them. The manual backtesting strategy has four steps which are listed below.

Step 1: This stage involves a trader opening the chart of the currency pair that you would want to backtest. A trader then scrolls the chart back to the prior period. It is easy to do this since one can change the dates on the charts by dragging and dropping. The trader must also make sure that all the indicators, as well as the other tools which are a part of the strategy, are available on the chart.

Step 2: A trader is required to move the chart from one bar to the other which will enable them to spot any prospective trade setups.

Step 3: After finding the trade setup which is normally based on the trading strategy a trader uses, the trader is required to note down all the results of the imagined trade that you as a trader have carried out. In order to make the process easy and efficient, one can use an excel spreadsheet. The trader will be able to easily enter the date, the entry points, and the stop loss column. They will also insert the take profit and reward to risk ration and any other additional information that a trader thinks that it will be of any benefit to them.

Step 4: At this stage, a trader is expected to repeat stage one, two and three until they get discover a probable trade set up. After going through all the stages, traders are then required to practice stage three for them to be successful.

Manual backtesting is said to be the most time-consuming strategy. It is also considered to be the best since a trader is able to participate fully in the process of backtesting. This way, a trader is able to experience how all the trading strategies are working in all the market conditions. The traders should not feel like all the effort is a waste of time since it is through the data that a trader will be able to tell if the trading is a success. Through backtesting, a trader will be able to have confidence in using the strategy when using it in actual trading.

For any trader to grow and develop their trading strategy, they would need to backtest. This is because backtesting will help in revealing how the given strategy will work out in numerous market settings. It is through backtesting that a trader will be able to tell whether the strategy is profitable or not. By following up on the strategy, a trader will be able to find out the areas that are experiencing challenges and find ways of overcoming the challenges. This will be of great help since the markets keep changing.

One strategy may be working at a particular time and may not work later. A trader will also be able to come up with ways of bridging the gaps in case of market changes. By doing this, the traders will be able to enjoy profits throughout the period.

Chapter 11: Strategies for Currency Couples

The Foreign exchange market (Forex) never closes. It works throughout the working week. People and business from every country in the world take part in trading in the Forex market daily in large volumes. This market has provided a system to promote the exchange of various currencies around the world and make trading possible. The trading in this market is all about trading-off currency couples form two different countries.

As a beginner, you may find Forex trading difficult, and you may find yourself becoming overwhelmed by a large number of currency couples that are available via different online trading terminals, hence get confused on the best currency pairs to trade. There is no forthright answer to this, and you need to spend more time, analyzing various couples and compare them to your strategy, so that you can determine the best currency pairs to trade.

In this chapter, we will focus on helping you to understand currency pairs, and aid you to identify the best currency couples to trade. This chapter will also explain the meaning of Forex majors and whether they can work for you or not.

Currency couples

They are also known as currency pairs. Foreign trade is about buying and selling currencies in couples. In order to buy and sell Forex currency, you need to know how much the currency in the pair is worth in comparison to each other. The link between the two currencies is what defines the currency couple. A currency couple is quoted using the currency abbreviations, and the base currency value. The base currency is usually determined using the currency counter, and there is an international way of determining how a currency couple is set up.

If a currency couple is quoted as USDEUR 1.54, it means that one US dollar is worth 1.54 Euro. In this example, the base currency is the US dollar, and the currency counter is the Euro. It is these currency pairs that are listed in foreign exchange markets. As a beginner, you must know how different currency pairs from different countries are abbreviated since it is these couples which get listed in Forex trade.

Understanding and reading currency couples

As a beginner, the first thing that you will have to learn is how to read quotes in the Forex market. Price quotes form the basis of understanding financial markets since it is the language of these markets. Every trader has to be fluent in this language in order to be able to pull through. At first, it will be quite daunting, but the good thing is that learning to read price quotes is an intuitive process and will not require much effort to master it.

Understand the quote Names

The name comprises the currency symbols of two countries which are separated by a slash. The symbols are called ISO codes. For example, The United States Dollar will be expressed as USD while the European Union Euro, will be shown as EUR .the firth two letters define the name of the country, while the third letter is the currency name. The Japanese Yen will then be written as JPY while Great British Pound will be expressed as GBP.

These two codes make a currency couple or the currency pair, and all currencies are quoted in couples. This is because for you to express the value of one currency, you need another currency to compare it with. Therefore EUR/USD is being used to determine the value of the Euro in comparison with the US dollar.

In Forex terms, it is quoting the Euro against the US dollar. In other words, it is expressing the relative valuation of the Euro in US dollars. The first currency, in our case, the Euro, is called the base currency. The second currency, in our case, is the US dollar. It is called the counter currency.

Many currencies that you will encounter in Forex markets are quoted based on the US dollar except a few minor currency pairs.

Understanding the quoted value

As a new trader, you need to know the dynamics of Forex quotes, and you need to know how to read the price of the currency couple. It is the price that will indicate the prevailing dynamic of the currency couple. It provides you with the basics to determine whether you should make the trade. Look at the price of 1.1233/1.1236 for the EUR/USD currency couple. These numbers indicate the base currency value (Euro) through the counter currency value (US dollar).

The number 1.1233 expressing the base currency is known as the bid price. It shows the market bid on the currency and represents what you will earn in US dollars by selling 1 Euro. The number 1.1236 is known as the asking price and expresses how much the market is asking for 1 Euro in US dollars in case you choose to buy. So EUR/USD 1.1233/1.1236 says that one euro is worth 1.1233 US dollars if you are buying, and 1.1236 if you are selling. This will apply to all currency couples and all financial markets.

Understanding Forex Majors

These are the major currencies in the Foreign exchange trade. They are the strongest and the most dominant currency pairs. They are the currencies of countries with strong economies in the world. Many people popularly trade them. As you would guess, the US dollar is the most dominated, the strongest and the commonly traded currency in Forex trade. This is because the US economy is the strongest in the world; hence, the US dollar acts as the reserve and the reference currency of the world in currency transactions. Foreign majors dominate Forex trading, and their liquidity is high. Forex majors that dominate financial markets currencies of the world's strong economies. Their values fluctuate in relation to each other depending on how trade volumes of their respective countries will change. Naturally, they are currencies of the countries with strong financial powers, and which have a high volume of trade in the world. They have the most significant fluctuations in price in a day hence being the most volatile ones in the Forex trade markets. Although they are the most dominant, they are not necessarily the best currency couples to trade. Traders can either make or lose money on the massive price changes, but they offer the best trading conditions, as they tend to have low spreads, but this does not make majors the best Forex trading couples. Due fo the best market conditions that they offer, they will be the best for beginner to help them mitigate losses and maximize earnings

Major currency pairs are based on a list of popular currencies that are paired with the USD. The basket of major currencies consists of 7 pairs only. These currency pairs account for most of the turnover of Forex market. For instance, EURUSD pair alone accounts for about 30% of the trading volume.

Overview	Performance	Oscillators	Trend-Following

TICKER 7 matches	LAST	CHG %	CHG	BID	ASK	HIGH	LOW	RATING
EURUSD EURO / U.S. DOLLAR	1.09809	0.09%	0.00098	1.09801	1.09820	1.09840	1.09642	⌄ Sell
USDJPY U.S. DOLLAR / JAPANESE YEN	106.771	-0.10%	-0.106	106.771	106.772	106.930	106.730	⌄ Strong Sell
GBPUSD BRITISH POUND / U.S. DOLLAR	1.2341	0.04%	0.0005	1.2341	1.2343	1.2357	1.2326	⌄ Sell
AUDUSD AUSTRALIAN DOLLAR / U.S. DOLLAR	0.67552	0.17%	0.00118	0.67558	0.67562	0.67620	0.67391	⌄ Sell
USDCAD U.S. DOLLAR / CANADIAN DOLLAR	1.33245	-0.06%	-0.00080	1.33245	1.33249	1.33387	1.33204	⌃ Buy
USDCHF U.S. DOLLAR / SWISS FRANC	0.99520	-0.33%	-0.00324	0.99515	0.99529	1.00078	0.99520	⌃ Strong Buy
NZDUSD NEW ZEALAND DOLLAR / U.S. DOLLAR	0.63247	0.40%	0.00249	0.63244	0.63261	0.63321	0.62962	⌄ Sell

Understanding the best currency pairs to trade

As a beginner, you need to know the currency couples that can potentially deliver excellent results for you as a trader. To analyze the best currency pairs, you need to know about the most popular currencies that dominate the Forex trade market. These are currencies of the country's which have massive economies and high financial power. They are the most popular hence the most traded, and they will be the right choice for a beginner because of their stability due to low spread.

You need to understand the currency couples that you trade better so that you can achieve excellent results in Forex trade markets. Among these dominant currencies, you can find a few currency couples, and by choosing them, you may make your trading easier since there is a lot of analytical advice and data available on them. You can use such data and information to make the right choice of a couple that is likely to win.

1. **USD/EUR currency pair**

    This is the most dominant currency pair and has the smallest spread among Forex brokers. It is less volatile, and it is usually associated with technical analysis. As a beginner, you can select it as your best Forex pair to trade, without too much doubt. A lot of information can be found about this currency couple, and help you from making rookie mistakes.

2. **USD/GBP currency pair**

    Massive jumps and profitable pips characterize this currency pair. It is a risky currency pair, but you need to remember that to make high profits, you also need to take great risks. This currency pair qualifies to be in the group of volatile currency couples. There is a lot of market analysis information about this currency couple, and many traders choose it as their best currency couple.

3. **USD/JPY currency pair**

    This is a major currency couple, and you will see it regularly in Forex trade. Its spread is low and almost has a steady trend in comparison with other currency couples. You may want to select this currency pair as a beginner as it has the potential to yield profitable opportunities for you.

Understanding special or exotic currency pairs

These are currency pairs which contain your local currency. It is any other currency other than the majors. The best couples for you will always be the one you have more knowledge in. It can, therefore, be of great value to trade your country's currency is, of course, it is not among the majors. It is only useful to trade your country currency if its volatility is good. Understanding the economic and political issues of your country will be a helpful base for you to trade Exotic currency pairs.

Such information can be found through announcements of various economies in Forex calendars. They help you to predict and forecast economic issues affecting different countries. Most local currencies will be quoted based on the US dollar, and you also need to have information about the US dollar as well.

Currency pairs of the developing countries

Exotic currency pairs represent developing countries as well as several developed European countries and are traded less frequently. The group of exotic currencies was formed by the means of the International Monetary Fund. Exotic currency pairs are usually highly volatile and are lacking liquidity. Note that this results in a higher cost of trading and abnormal price movements.

Overview	Performance	Oscillators	Trend-Following					

TICKER 67 matches	LAST	CHG %	CHG	BID	ASK	HIGH	LOW	RATING
USDBRL U.S. DOLLAR / BRAZILIAN REAL	4.0842	0.01%	0.0004	4.0842	4.0862	4.0844	4.0842	Sell
USDCNH U.S. DOLLAR / OFFSHORE CHINESE YUAN	7.12339	-0.02%	-0.00151	7.12300	7.12430	7.13092	7.11783	Buy
USDCZK U.S. DOLLAR / CZECH KORUNA	23.4170	-0.02%	-0.0049	23.4170	23.4229	23.4510	23.4131	Buy
USDDKK U.S. DOLLAR / DANISH KRONE	6.79977	-0.07%	-0.00469	6.79977	6.80066	6.80905	6.79756	Buy
USDHKD U.S. DOLLAR / HONG KONG DOLLAR	7.84212	0.02%	0.00123	7.84211	7.84241	7.84430	7.84070	Buy
USDHRK U.S. DOLLAR / CROATIAN KUNA	6.7520	-0.05%	-0.0037	6.7520	6.7620	6.7603	6.7520	Buy
USDHUF U.S. DOLLAR / HUNGARIAN FORINT	302.78	0.06%	0.19	302.80	302.95	303.05	302.36	Buy
USDINR U.S. DOLLAR / INDIAN RUPEE	70.9950	-0.03%	-0.0240	70.9950	71.0050	71.0190	70.7850	Sell

Understanding Forex CFDs

CFD is a term which means Contract for Difference. It is used to represent the movement in the price of financial instruments. Instead of buying and selling large amounts of currency, you can make a profit on the change of price without having to own the asset itself.

Understand the liquidity of Forex pairs

To make a profit as a Forex trader, you cash in on the spread of the bid price and the asking price of the currency couple. It is, therefore, a logical thing to know how much you expect the currency couple to move. The movement depends on how liquid the currency pair is. Liquidity is determined by how much the currency is being bought and sold at a given time. The most liquid pairs are those with the most demand and supply in the Forex Market, which is determined by banks, importers and exporters, business, and traders. Their movement on an average day may be anywhere between 90 to 120 pips for the most liquid EUR/USD currency pair. Major currency pairs are the most liquid currency couples, therefore providing the most opportunities for short-term trading.

On the other hand, exotic currency couples have less liquidity. However, there are many opportunities among minor exotic currency couples, especially if you have specialized knowledge about a given currency.

Understand Forex spread

The variation between the asking price and the bid price of a currency couple is what is referred to as the spread. For a currency couple to be profitable, its value will have to cross the spread value. A good example is in EUR/USD 1.1668/1.6669. The spread will be 0.0001, or 1 pip. Therefore when a trader enters a long EUR/USD trade at 1.6668, he will not be able to make a profit until the value of the couple is higher than 1.6669. So if a currency has wide-spread, it has to make a large movement to become profitable. In such a case, traders will have to trade for more than one day to realize a profit.

Therefore trading on currency pairs with a low spread will be appropriate for beginners, and it is usually the choice for most traders. This is because a currency couple with a low spread becomes profitable quickly, and make it possible to make a high volume of small trades, other than depending on large trades to make money. It is somehow better to avoid currency couples with a high spread. Experts recommend 0 to 3 pips. When the range goes beyond six pips, the trading couple becomes expensive and can lead to higher losses. All the same, you don't have to avoid everything with a high spread.

Chapter 12: The Importance to have a Trading Plan- Expounds on the Importance of Trading Plan

Forex is like any other business whatsoever. That means there are the ups and downs, the parties involved and moreover, there is planning to allow the growth of the business. The planning of a business is a very crucial thing the world of starting and continuing of the business. For great success then one must plan carefully and adequately for the running of the business. If the business is done without any planning then it is supposed to be a great wreck or disaster. So what makes business planning to be very important in any business or in specific the Forex trade?

Before we dwell on the importance of trade planning, what are the reasons why one has to trade plan? Trade planning helps one to set reasonable goals that he or she can follow. One cannot just jump into Forex trading without knowing what they end game is. One has to know how and why they must work hard. The investor just not have a way of getting things the easy way. He or she must get the success they deem by being able to observe their goals. The investor should set goals which he or she can achieve. The investor should know their limits and the lengths they would go to for what they want. So they should put something that sustains them as they work along. Goals are very relevant in any business they act as the driving force of the investors to what he or she wants in the end. Goals have been seen to work for all types of businesses if one is determined to get them. This means that they will also work very nicely for the Forex business.

Another reason to have a trading plan to work within the Forex business is to give a sense of direction. This is like basically the road that one has to follow to their goals. After the goals are set then the next step is looking for a way to reach them. That is where the sense of direction comes in. this is like the rhythm or flow one has to follow to their business goal. One has to think ahead and look into the future. It is like a journey and one needs a map for proper navigation. The journey, of course, is rocky but the direction has to be followed strictly. The investor has to be conscious of everything to ensure that one is focused on reaching his or her goals. The direction together with the goals give the investor purpose and also drive. Drive makes the investor move to the direction he or she is needed to business-wise at a fast and encouraging speed. He or she is supposed to make the road smooth by removing all the obstacles that are on it. Direction and goals in the business world will always go hand in hand.

A trading plan also allows one to be their own boss and take charge. Trading plans do not just come from nowhere they are made and formed by the investor. The investor is the one to devise the plan thus making him or her head of his or her investment. This is usually a big responsibility since he or she is the one who goes through the losses and the profits. So all the upbringing or uplifting and weighing down things are up to him or her. Once he takes charge of the whole business then success is guaranteed. That means the goals can be written down and the direction to these goals set. All these aspects are interrelated in this way when it comes to successful investing. The more one understands the aspect of being one's own boss and the good and bad things that come with it then one can be ready for anything that comes. This aspect is important since it helps the investor to know whether he or she can take the next step at their investment. If he or she is not ready to take the next step then one can say bye-bye to the investments.

The final reason is to increase the profits that come at the very end of the investment. Whether one chooses a long-term or a short-term investment the most important thing is the profit that comes after. Others call it a reward. This reward may be good or bad in short it may be a profit or a loss. Every investor gets into investments hoping and wishing that they get profits and not losses. Every investor aims at that from the start and they wish that they do not have to lose the cash that they brought in the investment. If one plans their investment diligently then what is expected is very fine results. This means that the profits are bound to be there. For-profits to come in this point there must be a set of goals which are closely followed by the direction one has to take and also taking charge is important. All these aspects still circulate the issue of profits and investments. Profits also come with great understanding of the Forex world. This means even the smallest and slightest details of this kind of investment. That gives a wrap for some of the reasons for trade planning.

When all is said and done the reasons for the Forex trade plan are similar to all the business or other investment. These are good things to keep in one's mind when they want to invest in the long run. The reasons are simple and easy to understand. They are however more than the ones provided and you can always check them out for a larger point of view. Trade planning helps to invest in a big way and is always a good idea to try it. So the next thing I will focus on is the importance of the trade plan.

The first importance of a trading plan is to invest wisely. Once one is adequately planned of their investment journey it means they are prepared. This being prepared means that the investor knows where his income will come from, how much he will use to invest and with how much time and finally he or she has already set goals. They help one in the art of preparedness and the facts that come with every investment. The investor is taught on how to plan for everything they do during this business period from the beginning to the very end. When an investor knows about his income to be used in investing and what way they will use it helps in the investing process. With a plan, the investor knows how much money to use every step of the way. It is advisable to use a small amount of capital first to see the results it gives to you. Then increasing your capital if the result is good is done over time so as to make a full investment to the business. This is a way to be careful during investing since it is easy to lose the capital one had.

The other is to understand the indicators fully. In Forex the charts have a lot of indicators one cannot deal in this business if one does not understand what the indicators mean. This is like the basic things in the foreign market. Without their knowledge then understanding then Forex trade is total darkness for you. They are easy to master. In any good business plan, the first things are always research. One cannot just dive in into things that they do not know about. One has to go back to the roots of an take up some information for the benefit of the investment. Any good investor will know that this is right and that he or she does not have to know everything they just have to learn. This seems like a very stupid and silly step but actually it is very important. If done right then the investment is bound to go well. On the other hand if done just wrong then the investment is bound to fail one way or another. It is very easy to make or break your investment by either following or not the protocol of understanding what you are getting yourself into.

The other is determining your assets. Assets are very crucial in the world of Forex trading. These are found in the indicators of the Forex buying and selling charts. This then brings us back to understanding the indicators on the chart. They fit perfectly on the plan on where one has to research on the investment they are taking. It is worthwhile to realize that the assets are the one's one to do each and every trade. They may be from the initial income or the initial income plus the profit. Forex trade is not possible without this aspect. While looking at assets is also important to look at the other side which is the credit side. The credit side is all about the debt or the loans side. It is important to understand the assets and the debts if one wants to invest in the long run of it all. Both these aspects matter in the world of business. If one ignores them they are bound to fully cave in their investments. Understanding both means one can easily know how to maneuver through as many situations as possible. So assets and credits are another importance in business too.

The next is to allow profits to come in and to avoid losses. Understanding of the market is very crucial. It is not just toying and expecting profits in the long run. The investor is to work on a plan that helps him or her become a better investor in the long run. Profits are something one must set a target for it to be their driving force. These of course land on the business plan. Forex trading is one of the easiest business in which one can gain the profits they so desire easily. The easy way is knowing what you want and going for it. The purpose of business is to earn a profit. This is the main and most important goal in the investment plan. If all the steps are done wrong then that means that the business is about to fail or go down the drain all of it. If the planning steps are done right then the profits will come and they will be bountiful. The main rule is following the trading plan all along. This is another great importance that every investor should know about when it comes to the trading plan and it's usefulness.

Finally, it helps one to decide on what to trade. This is very important since the Forex market does not just deal with stock. The Forex deals with shares and bonds. The investor should look at what he or she will trade-in. the most advisable is always the shares and stock since they are profitable if you know what you are doing. It is also wise to check the time frame one wants to invest in. that is either long-term or short-term which depends on the investor but the long-term investment is always advised to improve on the profits.

All these are the importance of a trading plan. It helps to keep the investor and the investment to check whether we like the idea or not. Making investment plans seem very tiring but they are worth it at the very end. Most people ignore these trading plans without knowing their benefits to an investment and to an investor too. The more you think about it they are the guide of both the investor and the investment to great success at the very end. The importance of a trading plan mentioned are only but a few and should act as a guide to understanding more of these trading plans.

Chapter 13: Tips and Tricks to Trade Like a Pro

Throughout this book, you have been able to learn some of the basic skills that will enable you to make it in the Forex market. However, that alone is not enough. To be an exceptional Forex trader, you have to be equipped with some tips and tricks that will enable you to maneuver around. You have to learn that best traders are disciplined and practice a lot. They don't just do trade analysis but also perform self-analysis in order to clearly understand what motivates and drive their trade. By doing a self-analysis, you will also help you to keep both greed and fear out of the trade equation. Here are some of the essential skills, tips, and trips that will make you trade like a pro.

Begin By Defining Your Goals

Before starting your journey as a Forex trader, it is important to have a clear idea about what you would like to achieve and how you intend to get to this destination. Ensure that you have clearly drawn your goals and mastered them in mind. After defining your goals, try to assess through the different trading methods available. Select the best method that fits you and ensures that this trading method will enable you to achieve your set goals. This is because each trading method has its own risk profile which will require you as a trader to develop some attitude as well as approach so as to be a successful Forex trader. For instance, if you are this type of person whose instincts does not allow to go to sleep when there is an open market position, clearly you are best fit for day trading. However, if you are this type of a person who is ready to take time and wait for some periods for trade to appreciate, then you are the best fit to be a position trader. It is appropriate that you be sure of your personality. Your personality must fit your trading style. Forex trading at times is stressful thus be sure that your personality matches the method of trade you have chosen.

Choosing Of A Broker And A Trading Platform

It is appropriate that you chose a reputable broker. I advise that as a beginner, start by taking a considerable amount of time to do deep research on the differences between the available brokers. Try to understand the different policies that each broker has as well as how each of these brokers goes about making a market. You have to understand that doing trade in the over-the-counter market differs from exchange driven market. Again, I advise that you be sure of the trading platform your broker is using so as to know the suitable analysis that will fit you. For instance, if you trade by analyzing Fibonacci numbers, just ensure that the platform your broker is using also supports the drawing of Fibonacci lines. Try to understand good brokers with poor trading platforms, poor brokers with good trading platforms and good brokers with good trading platforms. Ensure that you choose a good broker with a good trading platform.

Before Moving to Multiple Currency Pair, Focus More on One Currency Pair

By now, I believe that you have noted that the Forex trade world is a complicated world. This is probably attributed to the mixed-up nature of the currency market, the different goals different participants have and the wide and diverse characters. Unless you are a genius, it will be very difficult to understand all the financial and economic activities going around the world. Therefore, to be a successful Forex trader, it is important that you try to stick your Forex trade activities the currency pairs you are familiar with and have a good understanding of. It is an even greater advantage if you start with your nation's currency. However, if this is not what you want, I prefer that you chose the widely and most liquid traded currency pairs.

Clearly Determine Your Entry and Exit Points

Often many beginners are usually confused by when going through the information presented in the charts in the different timeframes. This is due to the fact that most of the times the information presented in these charts are so conflicting. There are times when what is shown on the weekly chart as the buying opportunity can be shown up on the intraday chart as a sell signal. It is advised that as a Forex beginner, if you have chosen to shift your trading to a daily chart say from a weekly chart, ensure that you synchronize these two charts. What I mean is that, suppose your weekly chart gives a buy signal, be patient for the release of a daily chart to confirm a similar signal. Just be sure to keep your timing in sync.

Study the Forex Market and Its Fundamentals

Having a deep understanding of the fundamentals of Forex market and the technical factors affecting the price action is of great importance. Without a reasonable understanding of the Forex market, you are likely to be affected by negatively. However, don't be afraid of the consequences of erroneous application or the consequences of failing to understand the technical or fundamental studies. Learning is a gradual step and as we make errors, we get to learn more. You must have proper money management skills as well as emotional skills as these play important role in the analysis. It is also appropriate that once you make profits, learn how to protect them. I suggest that if you have no skills in money management, learn. Money management will teach you how to minimize your losses and maximize your profits. I prefer that you develop a bible of money management and put it as trading library's centerpiece. This will guide you on ways of ensuring that you don't gamble with the profits you have earned hardly as well as cut your losses short.

Be Sure To Calculate Your Expectancy

Basically, expectancy will help you to determine your system's reliability. It is advised that as a trader, you should try to roll back and check your trade history. From here, get a measurement of your winning trades and losing trades. Try to compare the profitability of your winning trades versus the loss of the losing trades. For instance, you can have a look at the last ten trades you have made. Suppose you have not yet made any actual trades, I advise that you go back on your chart. Try to check whether the trading activities would have resulted in losses or profits. Now proceed to total the winning trades found and then divide this total wins. The below formula will guide you;

Expectancy $(E) = [1 + (L/W)] \times P - 1$

Where we have W and L as the average of the winning trade and losing trade respectively and P being the winning ratio percentage

Case Example

Having made ten trades, out of these ten, you have won 7 and lost 3, the percentage win ratio is $[(10-3)/10]$ which is equivalent to 7/10 (70%). Suppose that these seven trades earned you $4,200, your average win will be ($4,200/7) = $600. Again suppose your losses summed to $1,500, the average loss in the ten trades made will be [$1,500/ (10-7)] = $500. Now apply the use the formula we used to get the expectancy.

$E = [1+ (600/500)] \times 0.7 - 1$

$E = [1+1.2] \times 0.7 - 1$

$E = [2.2] \times 0.7 - 1$

$E = 1.54 - 1$

$E = 54\%$

This means that your system is likely to give you a positive 54% expectancy and your expected return will be about 50 cents per dollar you invest.

Always Begin With Small Sums

The best tip for any Forex trader wishing to be a professional trader is by beginning with a small account and then increase the size of your account through profits. Don't start by investing heavily. Don't be confused by the idea that larger accounts will lead you to greater profits. It is perfect when you are able to increase your account size through trading choices. Otherwise, I don't see the need of you pumping money to an account that will only lead you to strain your finances and emotions.

Focus On Minimizing Losses

Once you have made the decision to invest in Forex trade and you have funded your account, but it clearly in your mind that your money is at risk. Therefore, avoid making this trading money to be money used for your regular living expenses but rather look at it as vacation money. Develop an attitude in you that directs you towards trading. With this attitude, you will be psychologically prepared to accept small losses. This is a basic step in risk management. A trader who gives their focus on trade and accepts small losses are more successful than those who focus on constantly counting their equity. To be a professional trader, you must recognize the available markets. However, in order to recognize the markets, begin by first recognizing yourself. Assess yourself and be aware of your capital allocation for Forex as well as your tolerance to risks. Just ensure that they are not lacking or excessive. You have to master your financial goals and understand why you are engaging Forex trading.

Be Motivated By Positive Feedback Loops

By having trade plans that are well executed, you definitely will create a positive feedback loop pattern. As always, success breeds success. You will feel confident when the trade is profitable. Furthermore, take losses but ensure that they are small according to your trade plan. This will help you build a positive feedback loop.

Be Consistent With Doing Weekend Analysis

The Forex markets are usually closed on the weekends. When closed, take your time to have a deep study on the weekly charts so as to identify the patterns or news that can have effects on your trade. For instance, you may notice that a particular trade pattern is indicating a double top but the new and pundits, on the other hand, are making suggestions that there will be a reversal in the market. In the real sense, this kind of reflexivity could only be there to promote some pattern prompting the pundits to reinforce it. Therefore, be patient and according to your best plan, set up your things and follow your objectives.

Always Keep A Printed Record

When I began doing Forex trading, I always printed all the trade charts. Printed records provided me with a great learning tool. I would, therefore, advise you as a beginner to always print out the charts and then list all the reasons as to why you are doing the trade. List the fundamental reasons you feel swayed your decisions. In your printed chart, mark your entry and exit points. Also ensure that on the chart, you include emotional reasons for taking the actions you took. For instance, if you were anxious, panicked or you were just greedy, put them all there. By objectifying your trades, you will be able to develop strong mental controls as well as discipline that will guide you in executing trade in accordance with your system and not your emotions of personal habits.

Don't Give Up

Only risk what you can afford to lose. Forex trading requires commitment, determination, and persistence. You will not just wake up and become a trading genius within a day. Forex requires that you be patient and learn with time. Before giving up, ripen your skills and develop your talents as long as there is no pain in the learning process and the risks involved will not derail your future and life plans.

Always Automate Your Trading

It is appropriate that you should always try your best to automate your trading platform. I have already talked about the importance of emotional control. However, you can minimize the role of emotions by automating your trading choices as well as your trade behaviors. All you need is to ensure that your trading system produces similar responses to trading scenarios and similar situations that you would have provided.